Proposal Writing

Sixth Edition

Dedications

To Ron Coley, my husband, who is a wonderful, supportive partner throughout my personal and professional journey; with faith when I faltered, praise and inspiration when I doubted; and love and friendship always.

—SC

I dedicate this edition of the book to my wife, Lietta Wood, who has patiently read and constructively commented on the book for 30 years. Thank you for your patience, love, and support throughout this journey.

—CS

To Zohar, my husband, and Sonya, my daughter, who bring sunshine into my life, make me laugh, hug me tight, and keep me strong.

—YLS

Proposal Writing

Effective Grantsmanship for Funding

Sixth Edition

Soraya M. Coley

Cal Poly Pomona

Cynthia A. Scheinberg

Consultant

Yulia A. Levites Strekalova

University of Florida

Los Angeles | London | New Delhi
Singapore | Washington DC | Melbourne

FOR INFORMATION:

SAGE Publications, Inc.
2455 Teller Road
Thousand Oaks, California 91320
E-mail: order@sagepub.com

SAGE Publications Ltd.
1 Oliver's Yard
55 City Road
London EC1Y 1SP
United Kingdom

SAGE Publications India Pvt. Ltd.
B 1/I 1 Mohan Cooperative Industrial Area
Mathura Road, New Delhi 110 044
India

SAGE Publications Asia-Pacific Pte. Ltd.
18 Cross Street #10-10/11/12
China Square Central
Singapore 048423

Printed in the United States of America

Library of Congress Cataloging-in-Publication Data

Names: Coley, Soraya M. (Soraya Moore), author. | Scheinberg, Cynthia A., author. | Levites Strekalova, Yulia A., author.

Title: Proposal writing : effective grantsmanship for funding / Soraya M. Coley, Cal Poly Pomona, Cynthia A. Scheinberg, Private Practice, Yulia A. Levites Strekalova, University of Florida.

Description: Sixth edition. | Thousand Oaks, California : SAGE Publications, Inc, [2022] | Includes bibliographical references and index. |

Identifiers: LCCN 2021025081 | ISBN 9781544371535 (paperback) | ISBN 9781544371559 (epub) | ISBN 9781544371566 (epub) | ISBN 9781544371542 (ebook)

Subjects: LCSH: Proposal writing in human services. | Social service.

Classification: LCC HV41 .C548 2022 | DDC 658.15/224-dc23

LC record available at https://lccn.loc.gov/2021025081

This book is printed on acid-free paper.

Sponsoring Editor: Helen Salmon
Product Associate: Ivey Mellem
Production Editor: Gagan Mahindra
Copy Editor: Pam Schroeder
Typesetter: Hurix Digital
Cover Designer: Scott Van Atta
Marketing Manager: Victoria Velasquez

21 22 23 24 25 10 9 8 7 6 5 4 3 2 1

BRIEF TABLE OF CONTENTS

DETAILED TABLE OF CONTENTS

PREFACE

We are excited to provide this sixth edition of *Proposal Writing* and grateful for the book's continued success. We strive to improve the book while maintaining its uniqueness as the little book that will take you from being a new grant writer to being a successful grant writer. The book will do that.

It is an interesting time in the history of grant seeking—the United States is just working its way out of the COVID-19 pandemic, and the president of the United States, Joe Biden, is seeking to rebuild the infrastructure of the country. President Biden's goals include providing direct financial support to lift children and families out of poverty and establishing new funding opportunities for social, cultural, environmental, health and safety, and educational programs.

The philanthropic scene is also changing as more companies address the needs of the local community as well as offer support for national and international issues. There is a new creativity to address needs, to partner, and to involve those who will receive the assistance in the planning. In short, it is an exciting time and one that may certainly generate a plethora of grant applications through both federal and state governmental sources. This sixth edition of *Proposal Writing* will help you take full advantage of these opportunities. We want you to learn how to write a proposal that not only lets you compete but helps you stand out in the crowd and win!

We have listened to suggestions from our readers, and we have responded to them. In this book, the reader learns a bit of the history of philanthropy, about the types of funding that are available and how to apply for it, how to design a program or service, how to measure the effectiveness of the program through program evaluation, how to tackle basic research, and to develop a budget and understand basic budgeting concepts—all of this while learning how to present the material in a proposal format. We have included more examples and more samples in almost every chapter. And, in addition to having handout materials at Sage.com, we have included handouts in a new appendix.

Here is a brief summary of the changes for this edition:

- Updated chapter content

- More examples within each chapter

- End-of-chapter key points and activities
- New Proposal Sections appendix with templates and samples
- New appendix with learning objectives and suggestions for practice activities

Our goal is to continue to provide you with a high-quality book full of the components you need to write a winning proposal. We seek to stay fresh and current, and to this end, we are excited to announce that we have enlisted the involvement of a third author, a university educator who currently teaches proposal writing. Dr. Yulia A. Levites Strekalova adds current experience as a grant writer, manager, and teacher to our writing team, and we are happy to have her.

We thank our new editor at SAGE, Helen Salmon, for her expanded vision for the sixth edition to increase page size to facilitate including more examples, exercises, and activities. We are grateful to the many other people who have a hand in improving this edition including the following reviewers who offered excellent suggestions, most of which we have included in this edition: Thomas A. Artelt, The University of Georgia; Mike Butera, Bellevue University; Joy D. Patton, University of North Texas at Dallas; Ahmed Ibrahim, Johns Hopkins University; Joy Rubey, California State University Monterey Bay; Felicia Tuggle, Savannah State University; and Leonard A. Jackson, Georgia State University.

Proposal writers are in demand for government, research, education, commercial, and public-sector jobs, and grant writing is an established profession with its own professional practices and technical terms. It is easy to feel overwhelmed if you are new to grant writing or don't write grants often. This book offers powerful support. With *Proposal Writing* you have a step-by-step guide to conceptualize and write the proposal in a learn, explore, and apply format. By the end of the book, you will have skills and confidence to call yourself a member of the grant writing community.

We continue to believe that this little book has all you will need to write your first proposal, whether it is to a local foundation or to the federal government, and we are proud to be the ones who helped you.

Soraya, Cynthia, and Yulia

ABOUT THE AUTHORS

Soraya M. Coley is president of Cal Poly Pomona University. Prior to that, she served as provost and vice president for academic affairs at California State University, Bakersfield, and at Alliant International University, as well as dean of the College of Human Development and Community Service at California State University, Fullerton. She has nearly 30 years of higher education experience and has worked with nonprofit, community-based, and civic organizations on program design, evaluation, and grant writing.

Cynthia A. Scheinberg is a psychologist (inactive) with 23 years of senior administrative leadership in the nonprofit sector. She has successfully designed, written, obtained, and implemented federal, state, foundation, and local government grants. In addition, she taught program design and proposal writing for 18 years at California State University, Fullerton, in the Human Services Department. Now happily retired, she consults on program design, grant writing, and compliance issues and, in her free time, enjoys grandchildren and playing clarinet in two community bands.

Yulia A. Levites Strekalova is Assistant Professor of Health Services Research, director of educational development and evaluation at the University of Florida Clinical Translational Science Institute, and a grant writing coach for the National Research Mentoring Network. She is also a science and health communication scholar and actively participates in large federally funded projects as a program developer and evaluator. She has more than 15 years of research administration experience and has been teaching grant writing in the U.S. and internationally since 2014.

AN ORIENTATION TO PROPOSAL WRITING

A BOOK FOR THE BEGINNING GRANT WRITER

There is nothing more exciting or gratifying than to participate in designing a program, writing a proposal that gets funded, and ultimately, seeing that program come to life in the community! This book is written to help you, the beginning grant writer, understand the basics of grant writing and develop the necessary skills to write an acceptable, and hopefully successful, grant application. We avoid the use of technical jargon as much as possible and provide a step-by-step process to help you write a proposal for a nonprofit organization (including schools) seeking public funding through governmental or private funders. (For those of you writing research proposals, we recommend: *The Nuts and Bolts of Grant Writing* by Cynthia E. Carr [2015] and *Writing Successful Grant Proposals* by Robert J. Sternberg [2014].)

Grant writing is often the primary means by which a nonprofit funds its programs and services. Whether you are a person in a club or association, an employee in an agency asked to step up and write a grant, or a student taking a grant writing course, you will be challenged to enter into an open-minded, critical thinking process that will lead to a completed proposal. In this process you will be asked to accomplish the following:

- identify and state issues clearly and succinctly;

- understand and apply research findings to program design;

- design effective program evaluation to measure the impact of the program;

- listen well, work flexibly and calmly with others, and be open to the ideas of others;

- create and justify a budget for the project; and

- fit this within a predetermined number of pages and format.

Once you have learned how to write a state or federal proposal as outlined in this book, you will be able to tackle just about any proposal that comes your way. Plus, you will find that these skills will help make you a more desirable employee in the nonprofit sector or lead to a career as a freelance grant writer taking on projects for a variety of agencies. (For more information on a career in grant writing, you might want to consult with national organizations including the Association of Fundraising Professionals [AFP], the Grant Writers' Association, the Grant Professionals Association, or the American Grant Writers' Association. These associations help establish professional ethics and resources for grant writers, provide training and certification, and in some cases, help individuals find quality jobs.) In all, there are many things you can do with these skills, and we believe they are well worth learning.

We begin this journey with background information on the history of philanthropy and nonprofit agencies and then move directly into the business of writing grant applications and identifying funding for your program.

A BRIEF HISTORY OF GIVING AND PHILANTHROPY

The Latin word *philanthropy* is defined roughly as "love for mankind" (*Online Etymology Dictionary*, 2021). If you are working in the nonprofit sector, you are probably already aware that "love for mankind" can take many forms. Today, U.S. political orientations are on a continuum with those on one end believing that an individual's character is shaped by their ability to take care of themselves and their families without outside intervention and the other end believing that a safety net of social programs will enable persons who are in need to ultimately be successful. One perspective encourages individuals to "pull themselves up by their own bootstraps," whereas the other side seeks to provide a "hand up." Throughout U.S. history you will see the flow of giving surge and retreat based on the political party in power and their beliefs.

The history of giving in the United States has its roots in 16th-century Elizabethan Poor Laws of England that "were administered through parish overseers, who provided relief for the aged, sick, and infant poor, as well as work for the able-bodied in workhouses" ("Poor Law", 2012). Under the Poor Laws, persons who were needy through no fault of their own—such as the elderly, the sick, widows with children, and orphans—were cared for, whereas those who were needy but viewed to have caused their need, or perceived as being able to address their need without assistance, were fairly ignored. The ignored population included older children/young adults, pregnant single mothers, and criminals.

The Puritans followed the Elizabethan Poor Law model in caring for needy members in the community and took up collections in the parishes to meet those needs. Throughout much of U.S. history, benevolent associations were created as a kind of community-based insurance plan where individuals joined the association and paid dues that were used to help a family with illness or the costs of burial. These associations were established along the lines of ethnicity, employment, or religious affiliation.

The first grants made by the U.S. government were land grants providing the opportunity for citizens to obtain property upon which to build a home and put down roots. Bounty Land Warrants were provided to soldiers in the Revolutionary War in lieu of financial compensation. The Morrill Act of 1862 provided 30,000 acres of land for each congressional district that resulted in the creation of 69 colleges such as Cornell University and the Massachusetts Institute of Technology.

The late 1800s and early 1900s marked a period of explosive growth in strategies to meet community needs. In 1889, Jane Addams founded Hull House, a settlement house that accepted needy men, women, and children, and provided a range of services on site and advocacy for improved schools and services. Jane Addams and Hull House mark the beginning of social work as a profession in the United States. The following quote illustrates the struggle that even well-established nonprofit agencies can have in obtaining consistent funding. In 2012, Hull House was forced to close:

> Jane Addams Hull House Association will be out of business Friday, leaving employees and clients scrambling to fill a void the 122-year-old organization will leave. Despite announcing last week plans to close in March,

board Chairman Stephen Saunders said Wednesday that the organization will fold this week because it can no longer afford to stay open. He also said Hull House plans to file Friday for bankruptcy. (Thayer, 2012)

In the early 1900s, the first foundations came into being: The Carnegie Foundation was founded in 1905 to promote education and is the foundation that developed and manages grants for higher education known as Pell Grants. Shortly thereafter, in response to a desire to do something good with his money, John D. Rockefeller, Sr., established the Rockefeller Foundation in 1913 with a mission to promote the well-being of humanity around the world. Just as these foundations were created out of the wealth of individuals, so it is today with individual, family, and corporate foundations created to give back to the community per the desire and specifications of the creator.

In 1913, the U.S. government began collecting income taxes, and grants were made by the federal government to address critical needs and disasters. The country was well into the Great Depression in 1933 under Republican President Herbert Hoover. Hoover believed that the depression would eventually be resolved through legislation that supported businesses, and ultimately, when business was good, employees would receive the benefit in increased wages (this is called "trickle-down" economics). In March 1933, a Democratic president, Franklin Delano Roosevelt (FDR) was elected to office. FDR believed that the country needed more direct governmental intervention directed to the individual to end the depression. Through two terms in office, he created a New Deal with numerous programs including the Social Security Administration, the Works Progress Administration, the Federal Deposit Insurance Corporation, the Securities and Exchange Commission, and the National Labor Relations Board. These social programs provided jobs for the unemployed, put food on the family table, and spurred the development of a robust infrastructure of roads, bridges, dams, and other public works.

The next burst of social programs came in the 1960s under Democratic President Lyndon B. Johnson's "Great Society" when there was a flurry of social programs, including those to address racial injustice and the "War on Poverty." Another surge in social programs was the American Recovery and Reinvestment Act (ARRA) signed by President Barack Obama to provide financial stimulus to the states hit hardest by the Great Recession. ARRA's primary purpose was to support social programs and create jobs with $831 billion committed between 2009 and 2019. Most recently the U.S. government, foundations, and private companies issued COVID-19 pandemic relief grants. These grants provided an influx of funding for service delivery, community development, and basic research. As of the writing of this book in May 2021, the National Institutes of Health alone provided almost $5 billion for COVID-19 projects.

As you can see, particular social issues come in and out of style and face reductions or increases in funding based on the politics of the day. There is true variability in the world of giving. The types of programs funded by Congress are subject to realignment and changes in the focus of politics.

DIFFERENCES BETWEEN GRANTS AND CONTRACTS

To make some initial terms clear, the process of writing a proposal for funding has come to be known as *grant writing*, and the individual responsible for the writing of the proposal is a *grant writer*. The entity providing the money is called the *funder*. Although it is commonly said that one writes a proposal to obtain a *grant*, it may be that the end result is actually a *contract*. Be that as it may, we will continue to follow the generally accepted convention and continue to use the word *grant* freely throughout this book.

Contracts for services, or *fee-for-service contracts* as they are often called, require the agency to provide services on behalf of a funder, and the agency is reimbursed for services delivered. For example, a community dental clinic has successfully won a contract with the county to provide dental care to low-income children. The multipage document (the contract) signed by the agency and the county will spell out the details of the services to be delivered. In this example, the contract states that the clinic is contracted to provide 100 units of filling at $40 per unit, 10 units of crown at $500 per unit, and 100 units of cleaning at $50 per unit. The clinic bills the county in arrears (after the delivery of services) of service provided. If the clinic does not need five of the 10 units of crowns in the contract, they will most likely need to make a modification of the contract or risk losing this amount from the contract. In general, a contract requires a great deal of management to ensure that all services are delivered appropriately, services are billed and reimbursed appropriately, and timely changes are made to the contract to insure full use of the funds. (Find more on this topic in Chapter 10 under "Other Budgeting Issues.")

In contrast, we could imagine that this same clinic has also received a grant from the CSM Foundation, a corporate funder in the community. The terms of the corporate grant are that the agency will provide dental care to 100 low-income children. The grant does not quantify the type of care the children will receive, just that the funds will be used to serve 100 children. The agency will often receive the full amount of the grant at the beginning of the fiscal year and will report its progress to the foundation, making sure to note the number of low-income children served.

It is generally true that grants are more flexible in terms of what they will fund and require less detailed accounting of services than contracts. For example, a federal funder such as the Department of Health Services will not reimburse a luncheon for clients, whereas a private foundation like the Bill and Melinda Gates Foundation might easily approve the request to celebrate a milestone in the program and request a brief report on the luncheon event.

The process of seeking funding for the nonprofit agency opens the door to a rich and fascinating funding world that may include tapping into the altruistic drives of individual donors, following the vagaries of politics to understand and tap into governmental funding, and seeking to develop partnerships to access the wealth and influence of private foundations. The proposal carries the expression of community need to the funder, and if successful, results in a contract for services, a grant-in-aid, or simply, a grant. (Although there is a professional set of standardized terminology in the field, we suggest that you integrate whatever terminology the funder uses in the proposal you prepare. For example, the funder may ask for a "Project Summary," while we call it a "Project Abstract.")

DEFINITION OF A PROPOSAL

When writing a proposal, an organization seeks to receive financial assistance (an award) for its ongoing and future programs. The organization proposes a project or program that, according to the federal website Grants.gov (n.d.), results in awards to provide "support or stimulation to accomplish a public purpose. Awards include grants and other agreements in the form of money, or property in lieu of money, by the federal government to an eligible recipient." For funders, a grant award is an investment in a program with predefined activities and outcomes that support future positive change. By extension, a proposal is an application for financial support for a project that seeks (usually) to achieve specific outcomes and contribute to the resolution of a societal problem.

REQUEST FOR PROPOSALS (RFP)

There are grants and contracts available to fund educational, environmental, cultural, psychological, health and social programs, and services. Funding that comes through the government is known as *public* funding, whereas funding that comes through a foundation or corporation is known as *private* funding. Public funds are available through federal, state, county, and city governments. Private funding is available through foundations that are created to raise and distribute funds called *community foundations* or those created by corporations to distribute some of their profits into the community or simply those created by individuals to distribute their wealth through a family foundation.

In most cases, the funder announces that they have funds available to give by issuing a Request for Proposals (RFP). In some instances, you may see a Request for Applications (RFA), a Notice of Funding Announcements, a Request for Quotes, or other variations on that theme. The funder will often announce the availability of funds on their website, in newsletters, and through the mail. The RFP provides information about the following:

- the type of funding that is available,

- the target population,

- the topics to be addressed and desired outcomes,

- eligibility to apply for the funding,

- the amount of funding allocated,

- the source of funding and funder's goals,

- the format of the submitted proposal (spacing, typeface, and font, etc.),

- a listing of all documents that should be attached in an appendix,

- a description of the review process and scoring procedure,

- the due date for receipt of the proposal, and

- links to any forms needed to prepare the proposal.

The first thing you should do with an RFP is *read it carefully*. Take time to make certain that the organization is eligible to apply for the funds, that the target population in the RFP matches the target population you want to serve, and that the timeline is acceptable and doable. Get out your highlighter and mark the important information. The grant writer is responsible to know the details of the RFP down to the nitty-gritty of font size and spacing. Read and reread this document until you feel confident that you could explain it to another and follow its directions in detail.

KEY POINTS FOR CHAPTER 1

- Grant writing is an established and rewarding career path for those who seek to contribute to and improve society.

- Agencies use different types of funding such as grants and contracts to finance projects.

- Effective grant writers exercise flexibility while working with sponsors and developing proposals. They listen to ideas, learn the required jargon, and create in concert with others. They are attuned to and engage recipients in program design.

CHAPTER 1 ACTIVITIES

Chapter 1 Activity 1

Visit the website www.volunteermatch.org and search for grant writing opportunities.

Review volunteer opportunities. Note the tasks assigned to grant writers. What skills are required?

Use an online search engine like Safari, Yahoo!, or Google and search for job opportunities for grant writers. Note the organizations that offer positions for grant writers.

Chapter 1 Activity 2

Go to http://www.grants.gov and look for an RFP that interests you and read it. This will quickly help you understand the tasks involved in the grant writing process.

What components will be required to submit a grant? What terms in the RFA are unfamiliar to you?

UNDERSTANDING THE NONPROFIT AGENCY

ABOUT THE NONPROFIT

With few exceptions, the nonprofit agency is the only business type that is eligible to obtain governmental grants and contracts. The nonprofit agency can be known by many names:

- Public charity

- Not-for-profit organization or agency

- Nongovernmental organization (NGO)

- Community-based organization (CBO)

A nonprofit agency is usually established in response or reaction to a particular community need or issue. In its most simple form, the agency is created by a group of citizens who gather together, agree certain services are needed, write a mission statement, create a board of directors and by-laws, and submit an application to the secretary of state and the Internal Revenue Service (IRS) for determination on their nonprofit status. According to the National Center for Charitable Statistics, there are more than

1.5 million registered charities (National Center for Charitable Statistics, 2020a,b). In 2018, 63 million Americans volunteered in nonprofit agencies (NP Source, n.d.). According to Giving USA (2020), charitable giving accounted for almost $449 billion received from individuals, foundations, and corporations. Notably, nonprofits are a significant employer in the U.S. marketplace; they pay $634 billion dollars in wages and salaries representing nearly 10% of total U.S. wages and salaries.

Since 1913, agencies that are established for public benefit receive a designation of 501(c)(3) through the Internal Revenue Service (IRS). This designation means that the agency is exempted from paying taxes on the revenue it earns and that "none of its earnings may inure to any private shareholder or individual" (IRS, 2016). There is a common misunderstanding that a nonprofit organization cannot make a profit. It can, and if it is going to be a viable business, it must! This tax designation allows the agency to avoid taxation on its profits, but it pays regular payroll taxes on employees, sales tax on purchases (except on products used in resale with a permit), sales tax on items sold, and in many cases, property taxes. A viable nonprofit agency develops ways to generate income that can be allocated into a reserve fund. Many agencies will strive to have about 10% of their annual budgets in reserve.

From the moment of its birth, the nonprofit agency is on a hunt for funds to enact its mission in the community. The following are some ways in which nonprofit agencies generate revenue:

- *Events* such as dinners, auctions, picnics, dances, or pledge drives

- *Donors,* or those individuals who contribute financially to the agency

- *Corporate donors* that give funds through a grant process

- *Products* the agency creates and then sells, such as educational brochures or booklets

- *Clients* who may contribute financially to the agency by paying a reduced fee-for-service

- *Businesses* the agency runs that further their mission and generate an income

- *Grants and contracts* from local government, state government, and/or federal governmental offices

Most social service agencies will receive the bulk of their income through grants and contracts with their annual budget looking somewhat like Figure 2.1.

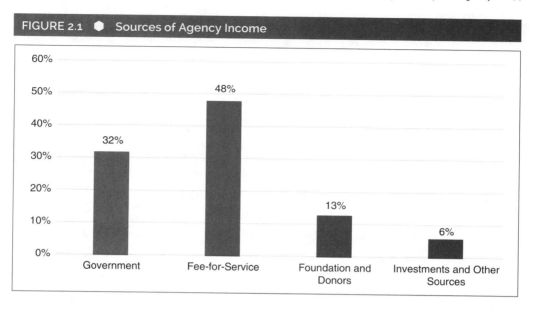

FIGURE 2.1 ◆ Sources of Agency Income

Each source of potential funding has its own rules and expectations in relation to the type of programs it will fund, how it will receive requests for funding, and the style of the proposal or application it will accept. (Every agency determines its fiscal year, which could be on a calendar year January–December; on a state budget year, July 1 through June 30 of the following year; or a federal budget calendar, October 1 through September 30 of the following year. An agency receives funding in whatever fiscal year the funder has and prepares reports accordingly.)

MISSION-DRIVEN ANALYSIS OF THE AGENCY/ORGANIZATION

In most cases, when you receive a Request for Proposal (RFP), the funder has stated goals and objectives, or a rationale for funding, which articulates the types of outcomes wanted as a result of the funding. An agency/organization looks for funding that is a match to its mission and current services and to the needs or problems to be addressed. The better the match between the funder's rationale for funding and the agency's mission and programs, the more likely the project will be funded and that it will be a successful project. In fact, it will be difficult for an agency to explain a request for funding that is outside its mission statement.

The first place a grant writer will look to begin to build an understanding of an agency is at its mission statement. The mission or purpose statement is developed by the board of directors of the agency (in voluntary agencies) or by other governing bodies (in public agencies), who create policy statements framing the agency's scope and its general approach to the broad problem. It answers the question "Why do we exist?"

Every agency's purpose is expressed in a mission or purpose statement that guides the agency through program development and community services planning. For example, Boys & Girls Clubs of America's (n.d.) mission is: "to enable all young people, especially those who need us most, to reach their full potential as productive, caring, responsible citizens". The American Red Cross (2016) mission statement is: "The American Red Cross prevents and alleviates human suffering in the face of emergencies by mobilizing the power of volunteers and the generosity of donors." Usually, the mission statement is fairly broad or global in nature, identifying the major issue the agency focuses on and a basic philosophy of how it is to address it. A mission statement may be so broad as to state: "to eliminate child abuse." Of course, we know that one agency cannot possibly accomplish this on its own; however, it tells everyone that this is what the agency is all about and that the programs will be created to contribute to the elimination of child abuse. The agency might develop parenting programs, provide a public information campaign to prevent shaken baby syndrome, provide educational programs in the schools to help identify children in abusive situations, or hundreds of other programs within the context of its mission.

A closer look at the mission statements can show whether there is a sufficient overlap and if a future collaboration is likely to be fruitful. For example, consider missions statements of two organizations that seem to have few connects at first, the Red Cross and The Weather Channel:

> *The Red Cross*: "The American Red Cross prevents and alleviates human suffering in the face of emergencies by mobilizing the power of volunteers and the generosity of donors."

> *The Weather Channel*: The Weather Channel leverages innovation in cloud computing to send billions of safety alerts each month, ensuring everyone can receive critical updates wherever they are, exactly when they need it.

The concepts from each of these short mission statements are mapped out in Figure 2.2, and now you can clearly see the overlap. In fact, The Weather Channel

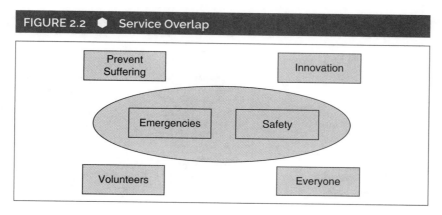

FIGURE 2.2 ● Service Overlap

and The American Red Cross regularly collaborate on projects like Weather Red Report, a weekly news segment that focuses on weather, emergency preparedness, and home fire prevention.

In addition to the mission statement, an agency may also develop a vision statement (and some add a values statement) to further describe their focus: for example, mission: to eliminate poverty; vision: every child receives a quality education and parents are gainfully employed; values: services delivered with respect and humility. To further elaborate on the mission statement and define action items, the Red Cross includes phrases such as "communities are ready and prepared for disasters," or "everyone in our country has access to blood" (American Red Cross, 2016).

It is easy to locate the financial statements for an agency because all agencies are required to file Form 990 with the IRS on a yearly basis. This form provides basic financial reporting as well as program highlights. When you view this document, you can see the funding received by the agency and the amount spent in any given year. You can obtain this document through the organization called Guidestar. org, which provides a searchable database of thousands of agencies, making it easy for a potential funder or interested community member to obtain a copy of the 990 and learn more about the agency.

The working agency is staffed with the executive director or CEO, who is the administrative manager overseeing the agency. The executive director is hired by and reports to the board of directors, who have fiscal oversight of the agency. The executive director hires and supervises staff, designs and implements programs, develops funding, provides for the fiscal management of the agency, ensures the agency is compliant with all regulations in their service area . . . in short, is responsible for the business. The nonprofit agency organization (org) chart looks like those of most businesses. There are program directors reporting to the executive

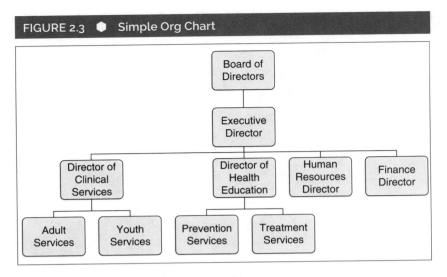

FIGURE 2.3 ● Simple Org Chart

director and service delivery staff reporting to the program directors, and so on. Figure 2.3 is an example of a simple org chart.

ORGANIZATIONAL CAPACITY

Reviewing the agency's purpose, its past and current programs, and its future directions is a useful process. The following "Survey of the Organization" provides a format for examining the agency, knowing what currently exists in the agency, and assessing agency strengths and weaknesses. The information you will obtain through this process will help you screen RFP to determine the proper fit with the organization as well as to develop a proposal that will move the agency forward with consistency and balance. We suggest you call an agency and ask if you can conduct an interview to learn more about what the agency does.

Survey of the Organization

1. Does the agency have yearly program reports and Form 990?

2. What programs does the agency offer?

3. What is the agency service area (geographic area)?

4. What population(s) does the agency serve?

5. Is the agency adequately funded to meet its needs, or is it struggling?

6. Approximately how many grant applications does the agency prepare each year?

7. Does the agency offer client-centered services that are culturally appropriate?

8. Does the agency have a way for clients to provide input into the services they receive or want to receive?

9. Is the agency open and comfortable sharing information with you?

10. Does the agency keep records of services delivered?

11. Does the agency conduct research to determine the effectiveness of its services?

12. Does the agency have a good reputation in the community?

13. Has the agency ever been in a collaborative? What services have they delivered in a collaborative, and what agencies did they collaborate with?

14. Request to see an agency organization chart (org chart).

Once you have completed this survey, you will have a better understanding of your agency, and you will be able to use this analysis to develop a new or expanded program that provides services in a realistic and manageable manner. Agencies are at various levels or stages within their focus areas, and your proposal must demonstrate an ability to reach a new level of service. Agencies, like any business, can overreach and develop too many products or too many activities that are not effective or sustainable. Too much diversity is a strain that can lead to system overload and program failure.

Consider the following example:

> An agency has been providing educational programs to youth in schools and now wants to develop afterschool programs for teens. The agency realizes that it does not have community contacts with youth-serving providers and is therefore missing a major link needed to advertise and obtain participants for the new program. It does not have sufficient space to mount the program; therefore, the agency does not pursue the grant to provide educational programs. To address this shortcoming, the agency submits a proposal that provides for a process to create these linkages and develop this new network to be able to provide the full program in the future.

Working With a Collaborative

The term *collaborative* refers to cooperative partnerships and liaisons for service delivery. In the past, agencies provided a set of services to their identified client base, usually across large geographical areas. Although these services were vital and necessary, they often were not sufficient to fully address the problem or meet the complex needs of the client. Furthermore, with agencies working in relative isolation from one another, it was difficult to know what other services were being provided and the costs of these services in total. Thus, the collaborative service model was born out of the community's need to do the following:

- provide coordinated and efficient services,

- address multiple and complex problems,

- contain costs, and

- improve access to services.

Beginning in the 1990s and continuing today, mergers became common in both the public and private sectors in an effort to bring escalating costs under control and to add "value" to products and services. Many nonprofit agencies either closed their doors during this difficult time or merged with other agencies. Agencies and funders began to look for new ways to deliver services more economically and efficiently as well as with more accountability for the results of services. It became common to hear funders use the term *outcomes driven* or state, "It is no longer good enough to do good in our communities. We have limited resources, and we need to know what works. And we must work together." Funders began looking at funding the nonprofit as an investment in the community, and as in the for-profit-sector, the funder seeks ROI—return on investment.

In the collaborative model, "communities" are redefined to better reflect actual interactive units of individuals, such as a religious community, a school community, or a particular neighborhood, rather than the broad geographical boundaries used in the past, that is, the XX County community or the Major City community. Service hubs located within the smaller community are created with an overarching vision of "one-stop shopping" for program recipients. These hubs are sometimes referred to as *family resource centers*. Agencies bring their services to the family resource center and forge linkages with the community surrounding the center, as shown in Figure 2.4. This model is more convenient for the client in many ways; however, there are often some services that don't travel well, such as medical services requiring expensive equipment or labs.

As you can imagine, a collaborative can be structured in many different ways. Another common service design is to locate services within existing sites in the community such as a hospital or youth-serving agency. Services from many

FIGURE 2.4 ● Collaborative Model Using a Single Site

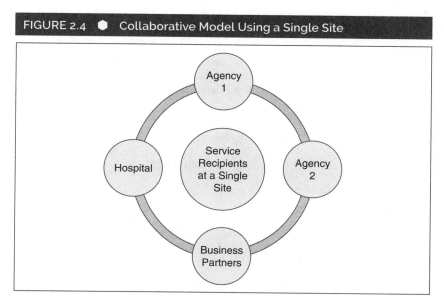

FIGURE 2.5 ● Collaborative Model Using Multiple Sites

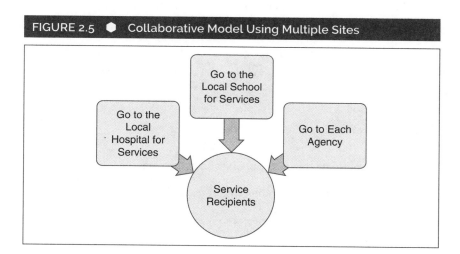

different agencies can be offered at these sites. Figure 2.5 demonstrates a collaborative in which the clients will be asked to travel to service sites to receive services.

As is the case with service delivery strategies such as collaboration, there are advantages and challenges. The advantages of collaboration include the following:

1. Better knowledge of what services exist in a given area and what services are needed (service gaps)

2. Increased effectiveness in meeting the interrelated and multiple needs of program recipients

3. More partnering among agencies resulting in new and creative service delivery plans—for example, the nutrition education classes of one agency delivered within the parenting education classes of another

4. Evaluation of the collaborative as a whole, providing the opportunity to see what difference multiple services make to a single program recipient

5. Increased access to program recipients

6. Increased ability to track the total amount of financial resources in a given geographic area

7. More flexible staffing through possible job-sharing arrangements among the agencies—for example, it may be possible to hire one evaluator shared by all the partners, or one clinical supervisor, and so on

8. The development of personal relationships among providers to facilitate referrals and future program development

9. Increased participation of program recipients in service delivery planning

10. Increased access to local data (studies conducted by agencies or schools) and shared past proposals to help write the need statement for current proposals

The challenges of collaboration include the following:

1. Significant time spent in planning and at meetings

2. The inability of some funding structures flexibly fund a collaborative

3. Potential problems among agencies regarding service planning and delivery structures

4. Sharing resources and taking shared responsibility for a mutual set of outcomes

5. Cost reimbursement issues if the lead agency is too small to manage the budget

A collaborative is a living partnership of people and bureaucracies. To be successful, the collaborative must have a shared vision, mutually developed goals, trust in the word of its leadership, a broad representation of collaborative members at the leadership level, and the ability to select and change leadership if necessary. Furthermore, the collaborative involves community members who receive services in important aspects of its functioning.

KEY POINTS FOR CHAPTER 2

- Nonprofit agencies are usually established to address and support a community or societal need.

- The agency mission statement focuses on the issue an agency wants to address.

- Working in collaboration with other agencies can increase the reach and impact of an agency.

CHAPTER 2 ACTIVITIES

Chapter 2 Activity 1

Conduct an online search for the mission and vision statements of a nonprofit organization. What core concepts can you identify?

Now search for mission and vision statements of a sponsor organization.

What core concepts can you identify? What are possible overlaps in the two sets of statements?

Chapter 2 Activity 2

Identify two to three other organizations addressing the same need as the one you are working on, and find their mission statements.

What are the similarities in the mission statements of all these organizations? What are the differences?

Consider using a concept map like that shown in Figure 2.2 to visually map the overlaps.

FINDING AND APPLYING FOR FUNDING

FINDING FUNDING

Sometimes grant writers are hired to write a particular grant application, and other times, a grant writer has the challenge of finding funding for existing or new programs and services of the organization or agency. Where does one look to find funding for community programs? If the agency is experienced and the ask is significant, grant writers start their research looking at government grants, both federal and state. They conduct online searches into government catalogues. Other small and large amounts of funding may be found through community foundation grants, smaller family foundations, and large and small corporations returning some of their profit back to the community.

Most funding sources have missions or mandates to follow. In the case of governmental entities, the mandates are developed through legislative process and administered by the governmental agency, and the resultant funding is allocated to address the identified need. Corporations and foundations also have funding mandates—some may fund community needs that are somehow tied to their products, such as a focus on health needs by pharmaceutical companies, whereas other corporations may target particular issue areas that their board or staff members want to address, such as after-school or day care services. This focus on issues can be used in the general search protocol looking for "foundations and issue" or "grants and issue."

In addition to helping the community, most funders also look for positive returns from their giving. In some cases, this may be increased visibility and goodwill in a local community; in others, giving programs can lead to increased revenue for the business. An example of this type of strategy can be seen in credit card use linked to charitable giving. If you use X card, the charity will receive a percent of your total purchase, thereby adding income to the charity. Individuals who want to support the charity obtain the credit card, thereby adding income to the card issuer. It is common to find that corporations are likely to view proposals favorably if they align with their own internal needs or promote the corporate image in the community. Of course, it makes sense to find a match that is a win-win for the agency and the funder. The savvy grant writer is aware of the WIFM rule—*What's in it for me?*—and seeks to design programs that bring clear benefits to the target population as well as recognition to the funder whenever possible.

Finding funding may also occur as part of your daily transactions with others—as you talk about the project, you will be amazed at how much people know about the topic and funding for that particular service. You may also find information on community giving in the administrative offices in the department store, bank, or grocery store you frequent.

THE FEDERAL GOVERNMENT

In 2002, in an effort to streamline access to and the submission of grants to the federal government, a portal called Grants.gov was established as a central storehouse for information on more than 1,000 grant programs and approximately $500 billion in annual awards offered by 26 federal grant-making agencies in 21 categories, as shown in Table 3.1.

The federal government usually provides the most generous funding and the longest duration of any grants or contracts available; in fact, some government contracts have a 3- to 5-year term. Plus, unused funds in a government contract may be moved into the next year in a process known as *no-cost extension*. Federal

TABLE 3.1 ● 21 Categories of Federal Grant Making			
• Agriculture	• Arts	• Business & Commerce	• Community Development
• Disaster Prevention & Relief	• Education	• Employment	• Labor &Training
	• Transportation		
• Energy	• Environmental Quality	• Information & Statistics	• Health
• Housing	• Humanities	• Food & Nutrition	• Law, Justice, & Legal Services
• National Resources Recovery Act	• Regional Development	• Science & Technology	• Social Services & Income Security

funds are highly desirable and fiercely fought for. When a governmental agency has available funds, they usually issue a *funding announcement*, which provides the information needed to obtain a *request for proposals* (RFP). (We will use the term RFP in this book knowing that a funder may issue a request for applica- tions [RFA], request for quotes [RFQ], request for bids [RFB], etc.) The RFP is the application packet containing the rationale for funding, full instructions, and required forms.

Funding announcements (sometimes called notice of funding announcements [NOFA]) for the federal government can be found on Grants.gov or in publica- tions such as the Federal Register at federalregister.gov or at the home pages for particular governmental agencies. If you know the federal division you want to apply to, you might go directly to its website and search. For example, you might know that you want a grant from the U.S. Department of Health and Human Services (HHS), which distributes the largest amount of grant funding of any federal agency (https://www.hhs.gov/grants/grants/get-ready/index.html), letting a total of 32,000 grants in all. The web page will direct you to look at HHS grant opportunities listed under Grants.gov, to search at HHS GrantsForecast, and to subscribe to their *Faith-Based and Neighborhood Partnerships Grant Information Newsletter* via email. (See Appendix B for Funding Resource Information.)

Federal government applications are generally prepared online through Grants. gov, which requires the agency be preregistered on the site, as shown in Table 3.2. Registration is a project that can take 4 weeks or more depending on the agency's familiarity with the necessary components. Once this preregistration is complete,

TABLE 3.2 ● Registering to Submit Federal Applications at Grants.gov
To use the federal government's grants management system the agency must do three things:
1. Register with Dun and Bradstreet to obtain a D-U-N-S: DUNS stands for Data Universal Numbering system that identifies a business on a location-specific basis. It is the standard business identifier for federal electronic commerce. It can take four or more weeks to obtain this number.
2. Register at the System Award Management (SAM) section of the federal government to designate an e-business point of contact (E-Biz POC) and authorized organization representatives (AORs).
3. Register with Grants.gov, where the registration application can be completed by the end of the session with D-U-N-S and SAM numbers are available for use. It may take a week or two to complete this process.

the agency can apply for as many grants as they want without having to resubmit this information.

Once the registration is complete, you can explore the online application. You will be able to cut and paste document sections into the application. You can also upload agency documents like organization charts, a list of the board of directors, a yearly Form 990, and other information requested by the funder. You can save your work on the site, edit when you need to, print and review, and when you are ready, print your final copy and send it electronically.

Many RFPs are being issued as online documents. Whenever possible, save the entire document to your computer, give it a new working name, and fill it in. Save an extra copy as backup in case you have a problem with the first. Once the proposal is completed, save it again as its original name, print out a hard copy to review, and if you are satisfied, send it back to the funder. Request an electronic receipt verification through your email software if possible and/or directly from the funder once transmitted.

In other cases, online applications do not allow you to download and are challenging to navigate, so take some time to click on all the tabs and understand the structure before you begin. Most often, the budget pages of these documents are linked to other pages, so a numerical entry on page 15, for example, may change an entry on page two. The best strategy we have found is to read the form carefully and put in some test numbers (note the page you enter the numbers on) to see how formulas are set and how numbers move around in the proposal. Once you understand the logic of the budget section, delete all the test numbers you entered and start fresh in the proposal. If the document must be filled in online, then perhaps you can print out the blank document first, prepare your answers, and then complete the document. Remember to check spelling, and be sure to print the document before sending so that you have a hard copy of what was sent, date it, and file.

THE STATE AND LOCAL GOVERNMENT

State and local governments get their money in the form of state and local taxes paid by residents and businesses, from investment income, and from the federal government. When the state has successfully obtained federal funding for particular issues (the state often has to write a grant proposal to the federal government for the funding), the state may make the funding available to counties and cities. This kind of funding is called pass-through funding because the money comes from the federal government to the state or local government and, finally, to the nonprofit agencies. Some examples of pass-through funding include Community Development Block Grants (CDBG), Ryan White Funding for AIDS services, and Medicaid funding. (Medicaid funding comes from the federal government to the state and consists of the amount the federal government will pay and the state will match. So, let's say, in California, the federal government pays 50 cents on the dollar with the county providing the other 50 cents of match to the state. To manage this, the county most often will require a grant application from the agencies who seek to provide Medicaid-reimbursed services in their jurisdiction, and they will develop a contract between the county and the successful applicant agency stating the services they are purchasing and the total amount available to the agency.)

Both state and city governments develop RFPs to enable competition for the funds; however, finding announcements of these available funds at the state, county, or city government website can be difficult. For example, you might want to start at your state or county website. For example, the state of California has a CA.gov/Grants website with some potential funding information but not all. Another resource that offers a more thorough listing of grants is GrantWatch.com (this is a subscription-based service), and for example, libraries may have grant-making resources, such as the UC Berkeley library, that lists grantors at https://guides.lib.berkeley.edu/az.php? q=Grants.

In general, you need to work harder to find the state and local funding opportunities. You will need to go to the departments of interest at the state level—you can find a list of all of your state agencies at your state website. For example, let's say you want a grant for your high school mathematics and science students. You search the website of the California Department of Education, and you find an announcement to develop a partnership between high schools and colleges and universities. You believe your school might qualify, and you read the application. You think it looks like your school and project are a good fit. Then, you call the program contact person listed in the application and discuss the program you want to propose to see if it is a suitable match. You have won if you come off the phone thinking that there is a good fit between the funder's goals and the program you want to submit. Plus, you have made first contact with a potential funder, and many times, the funder will remember you in a positive way and look forward to receiving your submission.

You might also search by topical issue and location and see what is listed, such as, *HIV/AIDS Sacramento County* or *block grant funding Oakland CA*. Each city involved in distributing CDBG funds will list the types of funding available and the application process on their city website. If you want to access county funding for specific services, it is best to call the county department offering those services and ask how you can learn about funding opportunities and to be placed on their notification list for new RFP. For example, if you want to provide drug treatment services, contact the county department of alcohol and drugs. You might also want to contact other agencies in the areas that provide the types of services you want to fund and ask what grant opportunities they are aware of or can point you toward.

FOUNDATIONS AND CORPORATE GIVING

According to the Foundation Directory Online (https://fconline.foundationcenter.org/), there are more than 234,000 foundations in the United States alone. The majority of these foundations are small and private or corporate foundations that focus their giving on a local or regional level (e.g., LA Arts Funders or Oklahoma City Community Foundation), although others are national in scope (e.g., Robert Wood Johnson Foundation, the 3M Foundation, or Bill and Melinda Gates Foundation). Yet other foundations may be national in reach but local in focus; this is most common for corporate foundations that invest in the communities where they do business (e.g., Walmart Foundation or Boeing Company Charitable Trust).

Community foundations are nonprofit under IRS designation 501(c)(3), and they can be both large and small serving a geographic area of their choosing. For example, the Southeast Virginia Community Foundation (https://sevacf.org

/about/what-is-a-community-foundation/) describes the mission of community foundations:

> to enhance the quality of life in the local area. Community foundations carry out this very broad mission by building permanent endowment funds and using a portion of the annual income to support a variety of local non-profit organizations through grants and special projects.

One way to find foundations is to subscribe to a database service that lists multiple grant opportunities by topic and location. Some of the paid sites have limited free usage or reduce costs depending on other affiliations or subscriptions the agency may have. Some of the most well-known of these are the Foundation Center Online at (https://fconline.foundationcenter.org), GrantWatch.com, GrantStation.com, FundsforNGOs.org, or GrantGopher.com. Some libraries and larger nonprofits subscribe to databases, such as ProQuest Pivot (pivot.proquest .com/funding_main), grant forward (grantforward.com), or Foundation Directory Online. Searches for funding calls (RFP) can be filtered based on the key words, funding type, sponsor, deadline, or location. Access to such databases requires a paid subscription that can range between $1,100 and $5,000 a year.

Grant writers in smaller agencies often ferret out grant opportunities by a) noting the corporations or businesses in their local community, b) going to the company's website and searching "community giving" or "grants", or c) conducting a broader search on the internet using key words like *community giving, corporate giving after-school program, grants for seniors, education grants, health grants*, or *community giving AIDS*, for example. Many foundations and corporations are open to receive proposals early in the calendar year until their funds run out. Other foundations set fixed schedules to receive proposals, usually on a quarterly schedule. You will find the schedules on their websites, and you may also find it has a simple online application for small grants up to, let's say, $5,000.

Once you have identified a company you want to research, look at the website for a section titled *Community Giving* or *Grants* to gather the details about their giving. If you are unable to find a link to the corporate giving program, use the *Contact Us* link and make an email inquiry stating that you are a grant writer for a nonprofit organization seeking grants for "your topic area" and wonder if they provide any funding. In some cases they will refer you to their parent company or a separate foundation.

As you conduct your search, you will want to keep information on each of the companies that look like they might have something for you. Take your time as you do this search, and learn more about the company as you search its site for the kind of programs they fund, what the typical size of the grant is, and how this giving furthers their presence in the community. Does the corporation appear to fund highly visible projects in which there is media attention giving a high public profile, or does the company tend to give quietly to the community in which it is located? Does its giving tend toward opportunities to involve its employees through volunteerism? Does it have a specific list of possible interest areas?

While you are at the site, take the time to learn about the corporation or foundation and what it does. How is the business structured? How many facilities does it have? What type of product or service does it offer? Who are its customers? Having a familiarity with the company will help you better target the proposal and help you make an in-person presentation to the company if asked.

You may also find a fairly thorough listing of local corporations and foundations at your local United Way. Some agencies become a member of the United Way to obtain funding for programs with United Way serving as a clearing house (it approves its members) and broker (it helps raise funds and supervise services for a percentage of the gross fundraising). An agency will go through an extensive vetting process to become a member agency and will also contribute to the fundraising efforts of the United Way organization.

CROWDSOURCED FUNDING

Much like a for-profit business would seek venture capital to develop a new product, the nonprofit sector is turning to the general public to support programs or even individuals in need through crowdfunding sites. Some of the crowdfunding sites are Razoo, Kickstarter, Indiegogo, CauseVox, and Rockethub.com. Crowdfunding came into being as a way for individuals to gather support for specific needs in their personal lives or communities. An individual may post a request asking for help to deal with an unexpected medical need or trauma, and strangers will reply and donate money to the cause. You may be able to identify a particular aspect of your program that lends itself to crowdsourced funding, for example, providing scholarships for needy clients, purchasing computers or other technology for clients, or providing seed money for particular projects.

Crowdsourced funding can be applied across a wide range of projects, from documentary movies to rescue programs. For example, in 2017, a film director and university professor raised $37,725 for his film *My Kid Is NOT Crazy* at (https://www.kickstarter.com/projects/1407649958/my-kid-is-not-crazy).

Although crowdsourced funding has some appeal for its ability to obtain an immediate response to a need, many donors still prefer to give directly to the nonprofit so that the bulk of the donation is used in providing the service, not in administrative fees, which are fairly high in most of the crowdsourced companies.

SEARCH AND REVIEW

Safari, Yahoo!, Google, Bing . . . these are but a few of the search engines available on the internet today. As you enter a few key words (the main words in your topic), thousands of references containing those words pop up on the page. (These results may be different on each search engine used, so check several main search engines in your search.) Learning to search the internet for relevant and reliable information requires a willingness to learn the language of search engines as well as the language of classification for the issue you seek information on. For example, you might enter *teen pregnancy* into a search engine only to find limited resources, whereas entering *adolescent pregnancy* yields an abundance of quality references. Experiment with a variety of key words until you find the most salient information. Search engines usually have information on the page to help you use their search protocol most effectively and are worth reading.

Whether you use a subscription database or an online search engine, the ability to access thousands of references in a single search will help you find new treasures in the form of current data or new funding opportunities. We recommend that you create files on your Favorites menu to store the addresses of these websites for your future use—files named, for example, "Funders," "Demographic Data on X," and "Research Articles," because it is all too easy to suffer from information overload when conducting searches. For a more detailed description of search engines and using the internet for research, we recommend an excellent book written by Susan Peterson: *The Grantwriter's Internet Companion* (Corwin Press, 2001). Another strategy to stay informed about upcoming funding opportunities is to subscribe to newsletters issued by the funding agencies. This is a good way to also learn about the programs and priorities of the sponsors you plan to target with your grant proposals.

IS THIS INFORMATION FOR REAL?

As you compile information through the internet, you will certainly find that some of it appears to be based in scientific fact and some is opinion, or worse! This wealth of information requires a degree of discrimination on your part. Which information is reliable? Is this a reputable source or a homemade website taking this opportunity to promote an opinion? How can you tell the difference? To begin with, you will find that most of the information that is valid and useful to you will be found on the websites of well-known nonprofit organizations (.org), universities (.edu), and state and federal government offices (.gov).

The following questions will help guide you through the process of identifying a reputable, credible source.

1. Is the article published or not? If it is published, is it in a respected journal? Are there references listed in the article? Do you recognize the author's name or affiliation? There are many opinion articles on the internet, so beware.

2. Does the site have product advertising and other pop-up ads leading you to believe that the information contained on the site is most likely to promote a particular product or viewpoint?

3. Do you recognize the name of the site as a reputable, trustworthy source for information such as the Red Cross, United Way, and the HHS?

4. Are the data referenced on the site attributed to a source? For example, does it tell you where the data come from, such as a study by the Centers for Disease Control and Prevention? If there is no reference as to where the data come from, be suspicious.

5. Does the website have the appearance of a quality site? Is it easy to navigate? Does it look professional? Is there information about the organization or company posted to the site?

Table 3.3 provides some reputable websites to assist you in learning how to identify a quality site:

Once you have located a few trustworthy sources of information, consult the references within each of those publications to find additional quality resources. You

TABLE 3.3 ● A Sample of Reputable Websites	
Agency Name	**Web Site Address**
Centers for Disease Control and Prevention	• www.cdc.gov
National Council on Aging's Benefits Check-up	• www.benefitscheckup.org
National Institutes of Health	• www.nih.gov
National Institute of Mental Health	• www.nimh.nih.gov
USDA Nutrition	• www.nutrition.gov
Substance Abuse and Mental Health Services	• www.samhsa.gov

Agency Name	Web Site Address
U.S. Department of Education	• www.ed.gov
U. S. Department of Health and Human Services	• www.hhs.gov
National Endowment for the Humanities	• www.neh.gov
Council on Foundations	• https://www.cof.org/

might also consult with a librarian who can help you find appropriate key words for your search efforts and assist you in identifying authoritative sources. As you look at several reputable websites, you will begin to see that there is information that can be verified, there are references to other resources, there is information on the author(s) and the affiliations of the author(s), and information on the company or organization. You will *not* see personal opinions, lobbying for political favor or office, or efforts to convince you to purchase something or link to other sales sites.

KEY POINTS FOR CHAPTER 3

- Searching the internet is an excellent strategy to identify funding sources.

- Funding may come from a number of different sources, including federal and state agencies, private and corporate foundations, or crowdfunding campaigns.

- The federal government provides significant funding for social programs but requires considerable effort to obtain.

- Community foundations are nonprofit organizations that seek to fund agencies serving an identified target population.

CHAPTER 3 ACTIVITY

Chapter 3 Activity 1

Write down one to two key words and conduct an online search using these key words along with the words "grant," "call for applications," and "funding."

What opportunities for funding came up? What types of sponsors provide funding related to your area of interest?

If working with others, write names of sponsors on sticky notes and post them on a board, or use an online board, for example, Google JamBoard. How many sponsors were identified? Are there any overlaps in the lists of sponsors?

THE PROPOSAL OVERVIEW

THE COMPONENTS OF A PROPOSAL

A proposal is a comprehensive communication tool. It enables the applicant to express the need of the local community, to apply local solutions to problems, to state the value of (and the cost of) the proposed services and the agency's unique ability to deliver said services. Much like the layers of a wedding cake, a proposal's sections need to fit and balance with each other. There are times when information is repeated from one section to another because questions may be similar—go ahead and repeat the information as the funder requests—this is often the case if the proposal is going to be "parted out" to reviewers who need some of the detail of a section but not all. The following listing provides a brief synopsis of the most usual components of a proposal while samples of each proposal section can be found in Appendix C.

1. **Letter of Intent:** Many funders will request a *letter of intent* or *letter of inquiry*, both abbreviated as LOI, in advance of submitting the proposal. This may be a request to assess interest in the funding opportunity so the funder knows how many applications it will receive, in which case, a simple letter stating that you plan to apply will suffice. Or, it can request that you send a synopsis of the proposal you plan to submit with a brief summary of the project and the budget. In this case, the funder will determine if your proposal idea

fits their guidelines and if they will allow you to apply. If this is the case, you will want to contact the funder's program officer (PO) in advance of preparing this letter to discuss the proposal ideas and to determine if the funder is interested. This will allow you to revise the plan to meet the funder's needs. After review, the funder will usually notify you in a letter inviting you to apply or rejecting your request to apply.

2. **Cover Letter:** A *cover letter* expresses the agency's interest in providing the specific services the funder has requested. The letter should indicate the agency's confidence in the attached proposal and the outlook of the agency toward a positive response from the funder. It may also include the title of the Request for Proposals (RFP), a number related to the RFP or project, the name(s) of the agency applying for funding, the name of the project for which funds are requested, a brief statement about what the project is and why it is important, and the amount of the request. The CEO or executive director of the agency and, in some cases, the president of the board of directors or other appropriate official usually sign it.

3. **Title Page and Abstract:** A *title page* is usually a form document provided by the funder in the application packet that provides the name of the applicant, contact information, and a brief summary of the proposed project known as an *abstract*. The abstract is often limited to 200 to 500 characters and is carefully crafted to present the project name, its general scope, and highlights of the project. It can be thought of as a mini press release on the project and should include enough detail that a person reading the abstract understands what is being proposed. Sponsors publish abstracts on their websites and use them in annual reports. An abstract is a great mechanism to promote the work of your agency and learn about the efforts of others.

4. **Need Statement (Also Called the Problem Statement or Case Study):** This is the heart of the proposal, and it describes the community to be served and the problem or need being addressed by the proposal.

5. **Project Description:** This section describes the project or program submitted for funding under this proposal. The funder will specify how to present the project as to whether it will be established through the creation of goals and objectives or simply through a descriptive process. The funder may provide specific forms for this section called *Scope of Work* forms.

6. **Evaluation Plan:** The funder will want to know how the applicant will measure the success of the project. The agency submits an evaluation plan explaining what the project outcomes are projected to be and how change will be measured. The evaluation plan will determine if the goals and objectives of the project have been met.

7. **Budget Request and Budget Justification:** The budget is developed to include detailed estimates of the expenditures of the project, and it is usually presented in the format requested by the funder. An additional budget justification document is written to explain how the numbers were derived and how the funds will be used.

8. **Applicant Capability:** In this section, the applicant describes its experience in developing and providing services. This section often includes a history of the agency, a description of past project success, agency staffing, agency board of directors, awards the agency has received, a link to the agency website for client stories, and an organizational chart.

9. **Future Funding Plans:** Many funders are interested in seeing how the applicant can maintain the project into the future perhaps by building in fee collection processes in the current plan or other avenues of income to support beyond this funding contract or grant.

10. **Letters of Support:** The funder is interested in seeing if other agencies or community members have an interest in seeing this project come to fruition. Letters reflecting community support for the proposed project from program recipients, community leaders, agencies, schools, or religious organizations are obtained and included in the application packet.

11. **Memoranda of Understanding:** If the proposal includes agreements between two or more agencies or organizations, most funders ask to see a written agreement from each of the partners or co-applicant agencies to be included in the grant application. The memoranda of understanding, also called the MOU or MOA (memoranda of agreement), is like a mini-contract stating what each party in the agreement will do and what they will be compensated and how.

12. **Appendix Materials:** This may include an audited financial statement, insurance documentation, the agency IRS determination letter, job descriptions, rosters, or any other documentation required by the funder. In some cases, the documentation requirement may extend to the partner agencies as well.

PROPOSAL SUBMISSION AND SCORING PROCESS

A funding process consists of several steps until the final outcome is determined. Figure 4.1 illustrates a typical process.

In many cases a funder will hold a *bidder's conference* designed to enhance the understanding of the goals of the funder and offer specific details related to proposal preparation. The bidder's conference provides the applicant with the opportunity to clarify the intent of the proposal and ask questions about the proposal in as fair a manner as possible. Prospective applicants receive a written transcript of the proceedings of the conferences held by the funder and of any questions they have answered over the phone. This provides a level playing field where all applicants have the same information. The conference also provides an opportunity to learn

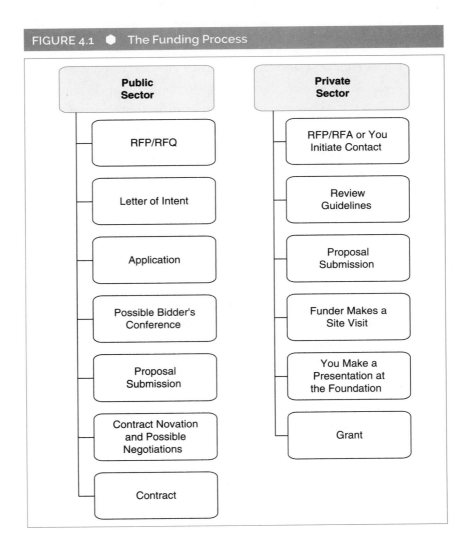

FIGURE 4.1 ● The Funding Process

what other agencies are interested in submitting an application, leading to possible cooperative proposals and assessment of the competition. It is customary for the funder to provide attendees a roster of all attendees at the bidder's conference.

The proposal must be received by the potential funder by the deadline date. Submission deadlines will be included in the announcement and will determine the time frame for proposal preparation. Many governmental funders allow approximately 4 to 6 weeks between the funding announcement and the proposal due date. Funders are serious about submission due dates. The funder will not accept a late application or any excuses. Any grant writer has stories of the horrors of being almost late or actually late with a proposal (which, in the case of a large application, represents hundreds of hours of prep time and potential lost revenue to the agency). One of the authors recalls missing a deadline to overnight mail the proposal to the funder, and she purchased a plane ticket for a staff member to take a red-eye flight across the country to get it there by the 4 p.m. deadline. Every agency has these nightmarish stories to tell. *Plan ahead* is all we can say. Give yourself at least one extra day of lead time to get the finished proposal to its destination.

An additional step in the proposal process may be if the federal government requires that the applicant notify the state government about the funding request they are making. It may be a request to notify your state senator or other political figure. The application provides instructions and describes who to make contact with and when. (This is sometimes called a *single point of contact* request [SPOC].) It may suffice to send a copy of the proposal to the SPOC when the application is submitted to the federal office. We also recommend that you send a copy to your local legislators so they might advocate on your behalf.

Once the proposal is submitted and it has undergone a preliminary review, some funders will make site visits to the agency to meet the board, executive director, and staff members to ensure that the agency is doing what it has indicated in the proposal. In some cases, the agency may be invited to make a presentation to the grantor's board of directors or staff.

Proposal Scoring

There is no single approach used for proposal review and scoring. Typically, government agencies create a panel of experts to review the proposal, and they assign points for each section of the proposal. The review criteria and the weighting system to be used are sometimes listed in the agency's program announcements or application packets. In reviewing the proposal scoring criteria used by public and private funders supporting human service programs, our survey found they generally weighted the proposal sections as shown in Table 4.1.

TABLE 4.1 ◆ Proposal Scoring Weighting System	
Proposal Section	**Percentage**
Need Statement	• 25%
Project Description	• 25%
Budget and Budget Justification	• 20%
Evaluation Plan and Logic Model	• 20%
Appendix Materials	• 10%

It is a good idea to study the weighting system in advance and to spend the most time and effort in the most heavily rated sections. Reviewers may meet together to discuss sections prior to assigning scores or may tally scores without meeting to determine successful applicants.

Foundations and corporations identify their proposal evaluation criteria in funding announcements but are less likely to indicate the point values assigned to specific proposal sections. The community foundation and corporate funder are more likely to use staff to review the proposals, whereas small family foundations may rely solely on family members. (We personally knew a family foundation member who opened the mail next to a 33-gallon trash can—interesting proposals went into a small stack, and the remainder went directly into the trash. This observation led us to focus more energy on producing beautiful cover pages on quality paper with border art, catchy project titles, and succinct abstracts for our small foundation proposals!)

Funders are looking for projects that are realistic, have measurable outcomes with a good chance for success, and are ambitious. It is always attractive if the program reaches beyond known boundaries into unknown or untried arenas, which if successful, will be a step into the future for the organization (and a nice success for the funder). Funders are especially concerned as to whether the agency can fulfill the goals for which the funding is provided.

In some cases, foundations may not issue formal RFP; instead, they will describe their area of interest and invite agencies to be considered for funding—these proposals are *solicited* by the funder who will not accept *unsolicited* proposals from just any interested candidate.

In addition to a well-written proposal, foundations give consideration to other factors in their decision-making process. We surveyed 164 foundations that ranked these as the top factors affecting whether an agency gets funded:

- Demonstrates a positive and measurable impact on those being served

- Is from a collaborative or partnership

- Indicates a cost-effective operation

- Supports other organizations in the community

- Reflects cultural sensitivity, equity, and diversity

- Focuses on primary prevention of the problem and addresses systemic inequities

- Has a proven track record

- Establishes new, innovative programs

- Receives funding from other sources

- Has a previous relationship with the foundation

- Has a not-too-radical reputation

- Has competent and professionally trained staff

In addition, the foundations revealed that two of the most common weaknesses in proposals are 1) not clearly identifying and substantiating a significant problem and 2) a lack of clarity as to how funds are to be expended for project activities.

Many times, one *well-placed* proposal has a greater possibility of being funded than one scattered indiscriminately to a variety of funders (also known as *shot-gunning*). Foundation and corporate development consultants are in contact with one another and are aware of a proposal that has been circulated in this manner—and may look less favorably upon it.

A *notification of award* is usually mailed to the applicant, and in some cases, the successful applicant may be contacted by phone. In cases where the application is rejected and the proposal not funded, it is often possible to receive the scoring and reviewers comments. This is helpful and strongly encouraged. On occasion, an agency may contest the outcome of the application process. Most governmental funders have a grievance process to follow if the applicant believes there is an error or oversight or wants to contest the determination. Details regarding this process will be found in the RFP packet.

In the best case, an award letter will arrive indicating that the application was successful and announcing the award amount. Sometimes this amount is less than applied for, and applicants will enter into negotiations with the funder. During these negotiations, the project description and budget sections of the proposal will be modified to reflect the level of effort required under the funded amount. Perhaps the letter the outcome falls into the disappointing column, and a rejection letter is received saying what a tough competition it was and unfortunately your application fell short. One of the most important things a grant writer can do is learn to deal with rejection. Attempt to learn why the proposal was not successful and learn from the experience. A rejected proposal can easily become the foundation for a successful proposal if you can tolerate the rejection and grow from it. It helps if you can know why the proposal was rejected because it can lead to being able to write a better proposal in the future.

KEY POINTS FOR CHAPTER 4

- Most common proposal components include letter of intent, cover letter, title page and abstract, need statement, project description, evaluation plan, budget request and justification, applicant capability, future funding plans, letters of support, memoranda of understanding, and appendices.

- A grant writer needs to be able to tolerate rejection and grow from mistakes. Cultivating this ability is key to a happy and successful career.

- A bidder's conference provides the grant writer with the opportunity to ask specific questions about the grant and meet others in the area who are also writing for this particular funding.

- The most common reason proposals are rejected is lack of clarity as to the program and lack of clarity as to how the funds will be used. A grant writer can hone the ability to write clearly by telling others about the program and seeing where they are confused or lose the point.

CHAPTER 4 ACTIVITIES

Chapter 4 Activity 1

Find an RFP or a call for proposals related to your interests. Note required proposal components and review criteria. Create a preliminary proposal checklist.

If looking at multiple RFPs, compare proposal checklists. What components are the same? What components are similar but listed under different names? What components are different?

Chapter 4 Activity 2

Find someone to share your proposal idea with. It is not too early to begin talking about it.

What ideas excited your friend? What required additional explanation? What suggestions did your friend have?

Chapter 4 Activity 3

Create a table with the first column labeled Major Problem/Needs and the second column Ideas to Address These Problems.

Keep your target population clearly in mind as you list items—in fact, it helps to put a picture of your target population in the center and add the needs and ideas around the picture.

LOGISTICS AND BASICS OF WRITING THE PROPOSAL

THE NUTS AND BOLTS OF WRITING A PROPOSAL

We are preparing you to write a big state or federal proposal. These behemoths will disrupt your life for a brief period of time. In most cases, you will spend all your waking energy writing the proposal up to the deadline. You will want to activate your support people and prepare your home and work environment to best support you. It helps to have a work area that will be undisturbed so that you can leave materials out as you work. A portable file case can hold materials and be used to transport information if you are working at multiple sites.

If you are the main grant writer, you may also be working with an agency administrator and program staff from your agency and at least one or two others from participating agencies if you are writing for a collaborative. The main writer pulls it all together into one style, ensures that all of the materials are gathered for inclusion into the grant, and makes certain that the grant application is in the format required by the funder. It is the responsibility of the main writer to read the Request for Proposals

(RFP) carefully and in minute detail to comply with the technical aspects of the proposal preparation such as font size, margins, page limitations, page numbering, and so on.

Plan to have someone edit and proofread your proposal. In most cases, this will be someone who has worked with the grant writer on preparing the proposal so there is familiarity with the project. In addition to checking spelling and grammar, the editor should help ensure that the main ideas in the proposal are clearly stated and that the proposal is internally consistent. All of the numerical totals in budgets should be double-checked by the editor as well. Finally, the editor should ensure that all attachments are included and the proposal is assembled accurately.

Although we have mentioned timelines that are imposed by the funder, the grant writer must also be aware of other processes the grant application must pass through before being ready for submission. It may need to be approved by the board of directors of the agency and partner agencies or the county board of supervisors. A board of supervisors, for example, meets monthly, so you may need to put the request in for signature before you have completed the entire proposal.

It is worth the time and energy it takes to ensure adequate supplies for the writing process in advance. Purchase extra printer, fax, and copier paper, copier toner, printer ink, stamps, large envelopes, file folders, pens, and large butterfly clips. Know where you can go to use a copier if yours breaks at the last minute, *and always back up your work*. Most proposal submissions are electronic, and you may be creating and getting edits on numerous drafts before your proposal is final. Services like Dropbox, Google Drive, and Microsoft OneDrive offer free cloud storage that you can use to set up a shared folder and organize proposal documents. (Remember to scan the thumb drive or other medium shared among users for viruses every time it changes hands from one writer to another before reinstalling the proposal on your computer.) Finally, make sure you have a copy of the final proposal—not just on your computer but a hard copy as well.

WRITING FOR AN ESTABLISHED VERSUS NEW ORGANIZATION

There is a vast difference in approach if you are writing for an established organization or starting your own venture. An established organization has the clear competitive advantage because it has a history in the community, has developed a successful funding track record, and has an established board of directors, programs, and staff. These are huge features to overcome in a newly formed nonprofit entity. If you are venturing out on your own, there are a number of features you will want to consider when writing your first proposal:

1. *Consider linking your program to an existing nonprofit with a similar mission.* Meet with the executive director and explore the possible fit. Develop a contractual agreement that spells out your relationship to the agency to protect your ideas and employability in the project once funded. Then write the proposal and use the existing agency's track record to reach success!

2. *Involve persons in the project who have obtained and managed grants or contracts over their careers, and use their experience and successes to build a credible foundation for your new entity.* This will help demonstrate that you have the capacity to manage a grant project and the capability to implement the program you are proposing.

3. *Talk to the staff at the foundation you want to work with.* Make sure that your ideas are a good fit and that the foundation will consider a *first* proposal.

4. *Demonstrate support for your proposal.* You must have solid commitments from partner agencies as well as from the community you intend to serve. This is always an important feature but becomes even more important in this case as you must prove that the intended recipients of the services actually want and will use the services.

5. *Consult as needed with staff in similar programs.* Listen and learn from their experiences, and build this knowledge base into the proposal. This will demonstrate to the funder that you realize that there are programs similar to yours and that you are willing to learn from them rather than reinvent the wheel.

6. *Establish a fair and reasonable budget.* Don't undersell the project, and set yourself up for failure and frustration, or oversell, and make your bid unrealistic. You want to come in *on target* with the budget request.

7. *Realize that your passion to start something new is both a blessing and a curse.* The same enthusiasm that will endear you to some will cause others to shun you because, usually, passionate people don't listen. Be willing to see your idea morph into something similar but also different from the original. Be willing to compromise to reach your goals. Remember, this will be your first program, and you can continue to build the dream over time.

If you are writing for an established agency, chances are good that you will be working in a small writing group or, at least, will need to obtain pieces of the proposal from others within the organization. The following ideas may be helpful to you in guiding the group grant writing process:

1. Establish the writing timeline early in the process and provide *due dates* to all involved. Make the date earlier than is actually needed to allow you time to bring it all together. Verify submission day, time, and time zone. For example, a noon deadline on Eastern Standard Time would mean a 9 a.m. submission cutoff time if your agency is located on the West coast.

2. Establish a tracking calendar for all sections of the RFP to include letters of support, grant components, and budgetary items.

3. Ensure that the principal person who will manage the grant is involved in the program design and reviews the budget.

4. Serve as or assign a primary contact with the potential funder. This will ensure that there is no lost or misunderstood information between the funder and the agency. Keep a written log of the questions asked and the answers received, and share them with the grant-writing group.

5. Allow enough time in the process to provide a final draft to all involved. This step can help fine-tune the proposal and ensure that you have a great product.

6. Enlist the help of one trusted person to make necessary copies of the proposal. Ensure the proposal has been copied and collated correctly, bound, and mailed with some form of delivery confirmation. Keep a copy of the mailing receipt. An overnight mail delivery system is the recommended way to send the proposal—both for the tracking ability and for the receipts.

7. Establish a protocol for handing off the project once funded. Continue to track reports that are needed for the project for at least the first year to ensure that the project manager is giving timely feedback to the funder as requested. Provide the project manager with a listing of the needed reports, their timelines, and the contact persons for the project. (This is above and beyond the expectations for most grant writers, but it is great for career advancement.)

WRITING A PROPOSAL FOR A COLLABORATIVE

When writing a proposal for a collaborative, the grant writer should be intimately involved in all phases of development to facilitate an understanding of the many aspects of the project and capture the richness of the effort. In some cases, the grant writer may be called upon to help develop the project and the proposal. One of the authors led a large collaborative for 8 years and has developed a model for conceptualizing proposals in a large group. The following provides a brief summary of the three-part model that can be used by the grant writer to help the collaborative members organize their thoughts and services prior to writing.

Phase I: Determine the Need and Establish Goals

In this phase, program recipients and service providers define the needs. At a meeting all together or through several smaller meetings, the community and service providers create goals and place needs under the appropriate goal. For example, there may be a need for immunizations and dental care in the community as well as a concern about gang violence. Two goals could be developed: one goal addressing the health and mental health needs of children and the second goal addressing community safety. The committee can make as many goals as they choose or use the goals provided by the funder under which local services can be organized. Once the goals are completed and needs fit underneath, ask the committee to rank the community needs from most important to address now to less important to address now. (The definition and ranking of needs will help determine the asset allocation to follow.)

Phase II: Explore Potential Program Offerings and Benefits

In this phase, service providers propose what they want to do to address the needs, indicate which goal area it fits under, identify expected results and benefits, develop a budget, and provide a rationale for using this approach. In other words, are there any data or research to document the effectiveness their approach might have on reducing or eliminating the problem?

Phase III: Develop the Final Program Concept and the Budget

The program offerings are listed under goal areas. The amount of funding requested is placed alongside each program offering. The column is totaled, and invariably, the budget needed exceeds the funder's allocation. Using the ranking system developed by the community and service providers, the whole group makes decisions about what stays as proposed, what might be adjusted, and what is eliminated from the proposal.

This process allows true collaboration to occur. In many instances, agencies are able to contribute some services *in-kind*, meaning that they will not receive money for these services; rather, they will pay for the services they are tying into the proposal. (By the way, some funders require a certain percentage of the proposal be in-kind contributions. We will address this issue further in the budget section.) Furthermore, in this model, all agencies are part of the decision-making process, and the *lead* agency of the collaborative serves as a facilitator of the process.

WRITING STYLE AND FORMAT

It is important for you to know who will be reading your proposal. Typically, readers of federal or state applications are professionals in the issue area of the request. They will know the jargon in the field and will expect you to use it freely and appropriately. (The Merriam-Webster dictionary defines jargon as "the technical terminology or characteristic idiom of a special activity or group.") When you write a proposal to a foundation or corporate funder who receives requests in many different topical areas, the reader is most likely an educated generalist who knows a fair amount about many things. In this case, it will work against you if you use jargon. Contact the funder and ask who the reader(s) will be if it isn't clear. Use sponsor's terminology to organize and reference sections of your proposal. Finally, if an RFP requires the proposal to have *Objectives* and *Project Approach*, don't call them *Specific Aims* and *Project Description*. Such inattention to sponsor guidelines will make the proposal stand out—and not in a positive way.

Although not stated in the RFP, proposals that are written to governmental funding sources and some large foundations require a formal writing style. Avoid colloquial words such *cool, great, kids, guy, amusing, awesome,* and *wonderful* and clichés such as "loads of" or "for many." In general, you will not use contractions, and you won't write, "I said," or "we think." Stay in the third person. Don't use abbreviated words like *T.V.* or *photo*—spell them out. State your points confidently and offer firm support for your argument.

To demonstrate what we mean by the difference between highly formal and a more "comfortable, friendly" writing style, here's a paragraph in which we say the same thing using each type of writing style:

Formal: The sense of community in Nirvana is enhanced through the presence of farmer's markets, greenbelt areas, and ample parking. Each member of the board of supervisor's dedicates one day per week at the marketplace, and the mayor and city council members do likewise.

Less Formal: Nirvana is a comfortable place to live with a weekly farmer's market, easy parking downtown, parks, and plenty of access to local government officials.

Just Wrong: It's lots of fun to live in Nirvana. There's just tons of things to do! You can go to the farmer's market and buy yummy fresh fruits and vegetables or chat with the mayor and other elected officials.

A proposal prepared for foundations or corporations accepting applications in a wide range of topics may accommodate a more comfortable, friendly writing style fitting a more generalist reader who will be familiar with the topic but not immersed in it. Typically, the proposal is written in a more journalistic style, such as an article in *Time* or *Newsweek*.

You will need to find the appropriate citations in the literature to substantiate what you are saying. Unlike a research paper in which you use footnotes or endnotes to cite references, the references are usually incorporated into the body of the text. For example, one might write, "In 20xx, the birth rate for adolescents ages 15 to 17 in Orange County, California was 38.5 per thousand (Orange County Health Care Agency)." Or, in another example, you may write, "According to a recent study conducted by the Children's Defense Fund (Annual Report, 20xx), latchkey children are at greater risk for stress-related disorders." We hypothesize that this style of referencing developed as a practical response to space restrictions; that is, with a limited number of pages in which to present a case, you are likely to resist devoting one to references.

In all cases, the final proposal should be a clean document free of spelling or grammatical errors. It should be visually pleasing with consistent section headers and typeface of a size and, if you had a choice, a font that is easy to read (think of the reader who has six of these to evaluate!). Charts, tables, graphs, and other illustrations can enhance the impact of the proposal and are now widely used. Avoid using shading or color graphs that do not copy well because a poor copy will detract from your proposal. (You may be able to insert shaded or color copies into each copy of the proposal in your packet if you think that the funder will not need to make additional copies to distribute to the readers.) Of course, if you uploaded the proposal to the agency portal, you need not worry about making copies for the funder, but do make hard copies of what you submitted for your own agency.

USING AUDIO/VISUAL MEDIA

Some proposals lend themselves to the use of short video productions imbedded in the text or sent in digital format with the proposal to the funder. This type of visual project can have a significant impact on the funder. These videos are usually short, no more than about 2 minutes in length, and focused on the clients telling a compelling story about a topic you are addressing in the proposal. It is often possible to find students who need to produce videos for school projects to help you to produce a short piece.

Most of the materials that you create should be protected by copyright, and we recommend that you check with agency administration before using or posting any images. This work will generally require copyrights, and it will be protected. Conversely, you should be careful not to take (steal) the work of others and put it in your project without getting permission or consent. When this is difficult or impossible to do, there are photos available in the public domain that you can use without worrying about copyright issues. The photos that you find in your computer software programs are open-source, and you can use them freely. You can also purchase the use of a photo from a stock photo store like iStockphoto.com, Shutterstock.com, or Getty Images. There are some free photos available from these sites as well. But be careful about photos that you see on the websites of others and do not copy them without permission. Any time you take a photo or make a video clip, you must have a release. We include a sample Photographic Release in Appendix D.

It is now a requirement that the agency have an attractive, effective, and up-to-date website that the funder can visit for more information. This site should have links to the board of directors, provide descriptions of the programs and key staff qualifications, have short videos on different aspects of service, feature the agency mission and values, link to annual reports and Form 990, and provide a clear way for persons to donate to the site. You should give your agency web address on all information pages and cite it in the Applicant Capability section of the proposal as well. (Remember to obtain permission for all photos used on the web page.)

It is a visual world, and it helps if you can break up text using photos or graphics and charts. This is said with a caveat in mind—if you are restricted in terms of the amount of space you can use in the proposal, you may not have room to add a graphic or other visual. Make sure that any visual you use can be copied and still be effective, and use colors or patterns in charts or graphs that can be differentiated in black and white print. Some basic types of useful charts include the following:

- Pie charts to show the different programs offered at the agency

- Column or bar charts to show the number of clients served by ethnicity or the population by ethnicity in the need statement section

- Organizational charts

KEY POINTS FOR CHAPTER 5

- Grant strategies for established and new organizations differ. New organizations should consider linking their proposal to an established nonprofit and involve consultants with prior grant experience.

- Proposal writing requires coordination within and across organizations. Checklists and timelines are useful tools for proposal writing.

- Proposals are written in confident, professional style. Proposals should also use sponsor terminology and key words to show attention to the RFP and knowledge of the topic area.

CHAPTER 5 ACTIVITIES

Chapter 5 Activity 1

Write three to four sentences describing the overall goal and specific activities of your project. Share it with someone and ask for general feedback.

What is the sequence of activities that you propose? How do the activities contribute to the overall goal of your project? What suggestions did you receive?

Chapter 5 Activity 2

Create a proposal development checklist for your project.

What writing tasks need to be completed? What administrative tasks are required (e.g., registrations)? What are the deadlines for each task, and who is responsible for completing them?

Chapter 5 Activity 3

Identify two to three prospective collaborators for your proposal idea and review information on their web pages.

What role could these collaborators have in your project?

What physical, technical, or social resources or assets could these collaborators contribute to your project?

6

DESIGN THE PROGRAM

> ## CHAPTER TOPICS
>
> Understand the Community through Data
> Formulating Program Ideas

UNDERSTAND THE COMMUNITY THROUGH DATA

A good proposal begins with the collection of good data. You need to make a case that clearly shows that there is a substantial community need that should receive attention. It is often not obvious to people why programs are needed and why your community should get money before other communities get funds. This chapter will take you through several steps toward understanding the problem and, ultimately, creating a program.

At this point, even though you may think you know what services you want to offer, it is important to keep an open mind about what the program might look like and let the data speak to you. The success of the proposal requires that you have a clear understanding of the nature of the problem you plan to address and that you have a sound approach for addressing it. The best way to reach this goal is to understand the factors that cause or contribute to the problem in the first place.

Have you ever gone without medical or dental care because you couldn't afford it? Have you seen homeless mentally ill persons pushing shopping carts up your city streets? These are examples of community needs because they affect the quality of life of the population in a geographic area. Other examples include: the incidence of HIV infection, the number of babies born with birth defects, the number of persons who go to bed hungry, the incidence of high school dropouts, domestic violence

53

or date rape, or perhaps, the quality of air or water. In short, there is a problem in the community that requires attention, and this problem is expressed as a need. In defining the problem, Kettner et al. (2016) state,

> A problem that is inadequately defined is not likely to be solved. Conversely, a problem that is well defined may be dealt with successfully assuming that adequate resources are made available and appropriate services are provided. Still, it must be understood that problem analysis is by nature more an art than a science. (p. 41)

They provide the following questions as a guide to problem analysis (pp. 43–47):

1. What is the nature of the situation or condition?

2. How are the terms being defined?

3. What are the characteristics of those experiencing the condition?

4. What is the scale and distribution of the condition?

5. What social values are being threatened by the existence of the condition?

6. How widely is the condition recognized?

7. Who defines the condition as a problem?

8. What is the etiology of the problem?

9. Are there ethnic and gender considerations?

Every community is unique. Think about the city you live in and those factors that define it—geographic, political, economic, and social components that make your city or town what it is. A quick visit to the website of your city will provide you with basic demographic information such as the number of persons living in the city, average age, average educational attainment, average income, and the number of children, working adults, and retired persons.

The following samples of data collection categories will provide you with a guide to the kind of data useful in both developing programmatic ideas and writing the need statement. You will want to obtain data on the following:

1. Incidence of the problem/need(s): whether the problem/need has increased, decreased, or remains the same

2. Clients' current physical, emotional, social, and/or economic status

3. Factors contributing to or causing the problem

4. Need in your target area to compare with other cities, counties, your state, and other states

5. Short- or long-term consequences of no intervention (including cost analysis if available)

6. Activities and outcomes of other organizations responding to the same or similar need, including any cost-benefit analysis

7. Demand for service: waiting lists, requests for service, lack of culturally appropriate services, and costs

8. Research studies on effective intervention strategies and evaluation results

Identify the interrelated components of a problem as illustrated in Figure 6.1—there are usually many components causing a problem, and these are often different in different areas of the country or among various populations and ethnic groups. For example, X Problem (e.g., homelessness) may be associated with Y factors (e.g., mental illness, unemployment, drug abuse). Social problems tend to be multidimensional, and there is rarely a single factor that explains the phenomenon.

The following section identifies sources that you can use to find for the types of data just described.

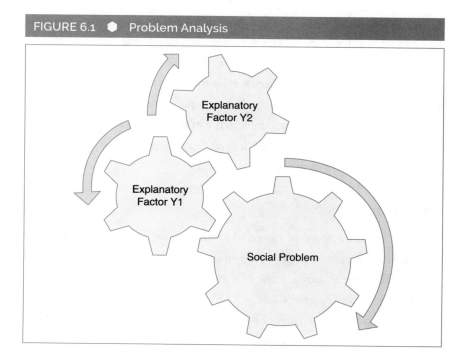

FIGURE 6.1 ● Problem Analysis

Client/Community Needs Assessment

A needs assessment gathers information about the client's/community's perception of the problem and needs. This type of assessment is usually conducted through interviews with program recipients, through focus groups, or with questionnaires. Many agencies have conducted needs assessments and may be able to share the results with you, such as a local health care council or the United Way. These documents are invaluable to making a case for your project. If you conduct an assessment on your own, it is important to involve members of ethnic groups (stakeholders) who experience the problem and who will benefit from the proposed program as well as individuals who serve this population. You may find that there are different perspectives on the problem and different solutions.

City, County, and State Demographic Data

Most county governments and universities compile information about the residents in geographic areas based on U.S. Census data conducted every 10 years. These demographic data provide information such as the number of adults and children, the number of single-parent households, the income level, the educational level, and housing density. Some university-based research centers have *geo-mapping* (geographic information systems) capabilities that allow a user to define a geographic area and extract demographic data and other indicators for that region.

Specific problems or issues are often tracked by county government and state departments working in those issue areas. Teen pregnancy rates, for example, may be found at the County Health Care Agency or child abuse rates at the County Department of Social Services. Community-based organizations will frequently have data already compiled on certain community problems. The most organized of these agencies will have the incidence of the problem at the local (city or county), state, and national levels. It is frequently necessary to determine how your geographic area's needs compare to other areas.

Journal Articles

There is a rich storehouse of information in scientific journals. You will find research into the causes of problems as well as research on effective solutions to the problems. From meta-analysis of the effectiveness of program designs to studies on a single program's effectiveness, you will be happy to see that there is a wealth of information on the effectiveness of different program approaches in various populations. When you draw upon this information and select a known and effective intervention, you are said to be using "best practices" or an "evidence-based" model. In addition, the bibliographies in the articles in academic journals can help a newcomer to a particular field find other important work quickly.

Local Newspapers

Articles in local newspapers can be another resource to help the grant writer develop a sense of the community perception of the problem and of local resources. (However, the grant writer must be cautioned not to depend solely on newspaper reports because their articles are only as accurate as their informants.) A local newspaper can assist in identifying local leaders and current events in communities.

FORMULATING PROGRAM IDEAS

The previous section of this chapter helped you think about developing a program with those to be served foremost in your mind. It also challenged you to look beyond your own ideas about what might be a good program idea and review the scientific and professional practice literature. You have also been advised to consider the capacity of the agency or organization to successfully launch the project and to think of ways in which all or parts of the initiative can be sustained post-funding.

You now need to refine your thinking and hone your ideas to formulate the specific direction you are heading with the proposed program. Similar to a funnel, you start with a number of ideas and directions that could address the need/problem (see Figure 6.2). You consider these in light of current resources, opportunities, agency capacity, as well as constraints, along with any parameters that the funder may have. Ultimately, you develop a program that you believe will achieve the desired results and address the need/problem.

As you read through the next nine steps, you will gain a good sense of the different components of the proposal. The following process will introduce you to new components such as goals, objectives, and implementation activities to name a few. We are going to take you through our nine steps to develop the beginning of a proposal and continue to expound on these steps in the remaining chapters.

Step 1: Understand the need/problem. Answer the questions: What is the problem? Why is this a problem? Who is experiencing the problem? Is it recognized as a problem/need, by whom, and how widespread is it? Are there social/political implications? What factors contribute to the need/problem?

FIGURE 6.2 ● Formulating the Proposal Idea

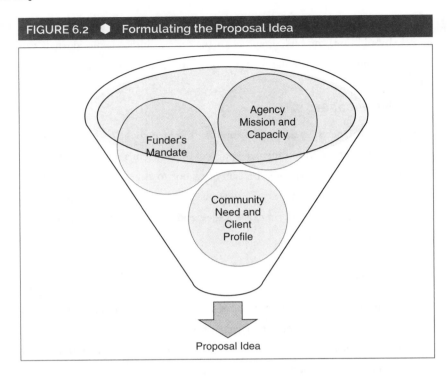

Step 2: Brainstorm solutions. Think creatively and freely about what might be done to address this problem. Dream of what might be possible and effective in creating change and positive results. Examine the scientific and professional practice literature to mine successful program ideas and use best practices when developing your plan. Consider the strengths and resources within your target population, the agency, and the community that can be coalesced to achieve positive results. Make a list of all of the ideas you and your team generate. Develop two or three program goals that are statements of the ultimate mission or purpose of the program you are proposing. (In some state or federal Request for Proposals, the goals are given.) Goals are often lofty and future-oriented statements such as 1) to eliminate birth defects in Grant County; 2) to prevent child abuse; 3) to make our oceans and streams pollution free; 4) to eliminate tobacco use; (5) to improve health outcomes in Grant County. The idea is to use a goal statement as a hoped-for outcome for a project. Goal statements are also used to identify major sections of the program, and it is useful to have three or more goals if the program is serving distinct populations or distinct types of service.

Step 3: Select solutions and describe results. Identify the best program ideas from your list that will achieve your goals and write these in the form of an objective. Objectives identify the target to receive the service and the *expected* results. They provide the "promise" of what will be achieved over the course of the funding period. Objectives are specific, achievable, measurable statements about what is going to be accomplished within a certain time frame, usually focused to address the causes of the problem. (It is also useful to think of objectives as the steps that you will take to reach the goal.) For example: The goal of a program may be "to eliminate child abuse." Objective 1 may state that "Fifty (50) high-risk families will improve family functioning by 25% by June 30, 2019," or "Twenty (20) abusive parents will increase their coping skills by 50% by October 30, 2019." Each program goal will have at least three to four objectives. (See more in Chapter 7.)

Step 4: Think about barriers. Ensure that the target population can participate as fully as possible. For example, a brick-and-mortar clinical services model to provide health care services may miss seeing clients who have no transportation to the clinic. Or another clinic may not be able to attract Spanish-speaking clients because there is no Spanish-speaking staff to greet them. The reasons why a client does not access service are known as *barriers* to service.

Barriers may exist as a result of a client's orientation to services wherein he or she may lack the knowledge, desire, or skills necessary to seek treatment or prevent a problem. An example of this type of barrier exists in drug treatment services when the client denies that he or she has a problem. The client may also hold attitudes or beliefs that are not compatible with the seeking of certain types of services. For example, an individual who uses traditional cultural healers may not value the services offered by Western doctors. Many times, however, barriers are created by the service providers themselves or through the program design and are usually assessed in five domains (see Table 6.1).

Step 5: Think about sustainability and the life cycle of this project: A funder may ask, "Do you plan to continue this project in the future? If so, how do you plan to support or fund it?" In the majority of cases, the answer to the first question will be "Yes," followed by a brief description of how the program may be developed in the future. The answer to the second question may be more problematic for the grant writer. Human nature being what it is, we are more likely to have fixed our minds on obtaining the initial funding for the project rather than concerning ourselves with the funding of the project beyond the current request.

If you view the question from the funder's perspective, you will realize the wisdom of this inquiry about future funding. It is nice to support projects that will do wonderful things over the course of the funding but rather frustrating to find that they simply cease when your funds are no longer available. From a funder's

TABLE 6.1 ● Assessing Barriers to Service	
Domain	**Relevant Questions**
Availability	Are services provided in the community, or are they cost prohibitive? Are the hours of operation convenient for the client?
Accessibility	Can the client get to the site? Does it take special physical needs into consideration such as handicap access? Is there transportation to and from the site? Are there eligibility criteria that may influence accessibility? To what extent are multiple services provided at a convenient single location?
Acceptability	Are the services in the client's language and sensitive to cultural issues? Is the staff perceived as friendly, professional, competent, and helpful? Is the decor and design of the service setting inviting to and respectful of the client?
Appropriateness	Is this the right service for the client (include cultural issues)? Will this service address the problem as the agency expects?
Adequacy	Is the service sufficient in amount and approach to meet the individual's or community's needs? Are services as comprehensive as possible?

perspective, it is reasonable to look for projects that have the potential to continue the work into the future.

You may know of other funding sources who will want to fund the project in the future. Or you may find ways to continue the project without funding, as in ways to "institutionalize" your project, meaning to imbed it into existing service delivery systems such as schools, hospitals, churches, or other agency services. Or, you may explore whether the project has the ability to receive income from the project itself, building a way to support the project later on. Ask the following questions:

- Can the program charge a fee-for-service or receive a donation from the clients?

- Is it possible to market products or materials developed under the project to other agencies or businesses?

- Can the agency turn the program into a service that the community at-large will pay to receive?

Step 6: Determine tasks to accomplish solutions. These are known as *implementation activities.* There are two kinds: activities that are preparatory to starting a program and activities that describe the deliverable or promise of each objective. As the preceding objective says: Fifty (50) high-risk families will improve family functioning by 25% by June 30, 2020, and an implementation activity will describe the services that the families will receive to reach this objective, for example, a 12-week educational program on family communication skills.

Preparatory activities prior to the start of services include the following: the staff needs to be recruited and hired, participants need to be located and recruited for service, facilities need to be identified and prepared, and program materials need to be created or ordered. Once the program starts, activities include the actual services as scheduled and delivered, tracking and documentation of client participation, and program evaluation conducted on schedule and in the prescribed manner (more on this in Chapter 7).

Step 7: Estimate resources needed. What are the resources needed in both human and monetary terms? What do you estimate the proposed program components will cost? Will the total available funds be sufficient to cover the cost of the project? Although we encourage free thinking to generate proposal ideas, it is time to ground in reality. Take some time now to briefly assess the cost of what is being proposed (more detail on this is in Chapter 10). Take a quick look at the big ticket items: staffing, rent, and indirect costs. Estimate the cost. Revise the program accordingly.

For example: You are writing a proposal for a $20,000 foundation grant. You want to offer an after-school program from 3 p.m. to 5 p.m., 5 days a week for 12 weeks for 25 youth. You want to contract a credentialed teacher, a physical education (PE) instructor, and a counselor to be present the entire time. The rate for the teacher is $100/hour times 10 hours for $1,000/week or $12,000 per summer. The PE instructor is $50/hour times 10 hours for $500/week or $6,000, and the counselor is $80/hour times 10 hours for $800/week or $9,600. You can quickly see that the design is not supportable.

You might want to solicit in-kind donations—which is when products or services are donated to the agency—to reduce the amount of funding requested. For example, if the project plans to publish a newsletter, you can find a local printer who will provide a donation of printing to the agency. Or, you might receive a donation in the form of books, office supplies, or furniture. People may donate their time and skills to the program in-kind, which can be counted as funds to offset the grantors funds. (See Chapter 10 for more on this topic.)

Step 8: Make necessary adjustments to solutions and benefits. The hard reality is that most of the time, we think of programs that cost more than the available funding, or we find an insurmountable barrier or other problem in implementation. We have to make some adjustments in the project. Try not to let yourself be discouraged by this—the ideas may be used in future programs and services.

Step 9: Identify measurement of outcomes. How will we measure success? What evidence is needed to determine whether we have been successful? We have said that we will improve family functioning, increase knowledge, and build skills. We will determine what we will use to measure success such as pre- and posttests, standardized tests, or observation, for example. We will address this in greater detail in Chapter 7.)

Figure 6.3 summarizes the process of developing a program as you identify the problem, develop approaches or services, conceptualize measurable outcomes, reassess the impact on the problem, and either keep or modify the plan.

Once you have completed these steps, you will have developed a substantial program. The authors have always felt that we could improve upon the program designs we have created, no matter how many times we returned to it. There is always something that can be improved upon. However, there comes a time when you will want to let it go and move on. Once a program is funded and you have the opportunity to see it in action, you will bring new ideas and improvements to future iterations of the project.

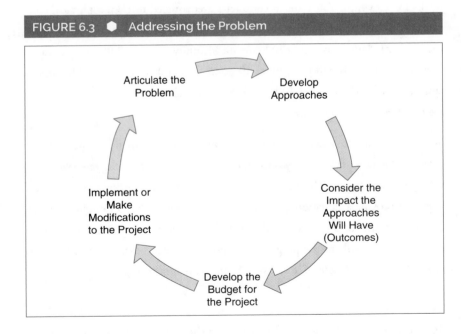

FIGURE 6.3 ● Addressing the Problem

KEY POINTS FOR CHAPTER 6

1. Systematic problem analysis is an essential step in proposal writing.

2. Needs assessments, demographic and census data, local and regional records, and publications are sources of data used by proposal writers.

3. Proposal development is a sequence of steps that includes idea development, selection of a solution, consideration of possible barriers, mapping out of tasks, and planning of evaluation.

CHAPTER 6 ACTIVITIES

Chapter 6 Activity 1

Write the top three needs your proposal addresses.

What data supports the needs you have identified?

Chapter 6 Activity 2

Talk about your proposal and the needs it will address to someone.

How easy was it for you to talk about the significance of your project? Identify two challenges you have in explaining the needs to others.

Generate two solutions or ideas that will help you explain the needs more succinctly. Share the new statements with someone and get feedback.

Chapter 6 Activity 3

What are the multitude of factors that contribute to the need/problem/issue? Identify in each category (as applicable):

   a. Individual/Family Factors

   b. Community/Environmental Factors

   c. Institutional Factors

   d. Systemic/Societal Factors

What is the vision or desired state if this need/problem/issue is addressed?

Share your work with someone. Ask for comments about the strengths and weaknesses of the presented arguments.

7

PROGRAM OBJECTIVES AND EVALUATION

CHAPTER TOPICS

Evaluation

Four Steps to Preparing the Objectives and Evaluation Plan

A Logic Model

Writing the Evaluation Section

Ethical Considerations

EVALUATION

You can't go too far in thinking about a program without considering what changes the program may bring about in the client, the community, and even the provider. When submitting a proposal you will be expected to prepare the evaluation plan following your description of the proposed project. By placing this chapter here, we are trying to provide you with the opportunity to be aware of the impact the evaluation may have on the program design. We want you to understand that the evaluation plan is tied to the project's goals and objectives.

When you design an evaluation plan, you are seeking to determine whether the stated project components or objectives were achieved. The objectives represent the "promise," and the evaluation provides evidence that the promise was fulfilled. In this chapter, we will focus on *process* and *outcome* evaluation. Evaluation is a core project activity. When planning a project, make sure to include evaluation tasks on the project timeline, and allocate sufficient time for evaluation data collection and analysis. (If you need additional help seeing how the project ties to evaluation, you may want to read the "Program Design and Evaluation Case Study" in Appendix D.)

A process evaluation provides an assessment of the procedures used in conducting the program, hence the term "process" rather than "outcome." A primary goal of this type of evaluation is to gather feedback information during the operation of the program to determine how the service was delivered or how the client was recruited. For example, let's say you want to know which outreach efforts result in getting the most people into programs: phone calls, flyers, directory listings, websites, newspaper articles, or other forms of outreach. Conducting this type of research may include the following:

- one-on-one interview of participants of the program,

- detailed tracking of staff efforts in outreach efforts,

- assessment of administrative and programmatic functions and activities, and

- detailed accounting of how each participant heard of the program.

The results can be used to improve the implementation of a subsequent program with a similar focus. Process evaluation provides an understanding of how you achieved the results; that is, it describes what happened, how the activities were accomplished, and at what level of effort. When you conduct a process evaluation, the objective is written to indicate a process evaluation is needed. So simply stated, there are process objectives and process evaluations.

Process evaluations can be written, for example, on the following:

Training or Education Programs

1. What is content of the training? What are the unique features of the training?

2. How is the training conducted? What procedures, techniques, materials, and products are used? What is the background of the trainer(s)? What costs are associated with the training?

3. What is the background of individuals trained, and which training techniques are most effective with which groups?

4. What are the staff's perceptions of the quality of the training? How can it be improved? What level of effort is required to accomplish each facet of the training?

Products/Materials Development

1. What and how are the products/materials developed and tested?

2. How are the products/materials disseminated?

3. How are the products used, including how often, by whom, by how many?

4. What are user and staff perceptions about the products/materials?

5. What is the cost savings associated with the products/materials?

Improving Operations or Procedures

1. What is the nature of the improved operations or procedures? How do they contrast with the previous ones?

2. What is the implementation process for the new procedures or operations?

3. How do the new procedures or operations affect service? Contrast cost savings and level of effort between old and new.

Although process evaluation can be valuable in understanding how things work and how things can be improved, the reality is that they are used infrequently due to cost constraints.

The most common type of program evaluation is known as outcome evaluation that determines how well the program achieved its objectives. An outcome evaluation focuses on these questions: "What or how much was achieved? What changes occurred in program participants or community conditions?" This type of evaluation is sometimes referred to as the "so what" of the program; that is, so what happened, so what was accomplished, so what difference did it make? The following illustrates the conceptual framework for developing a results-based outcome evaluation plan (see Figure 7.1).

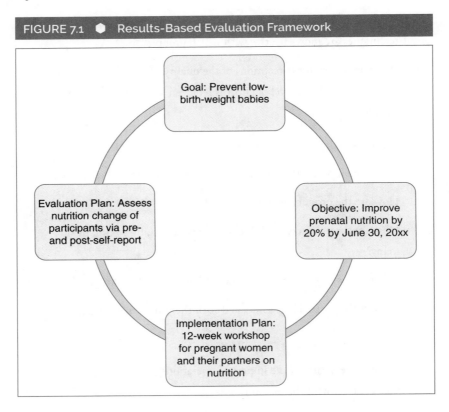

FIGURE 7.1 ● Results-Based Evaluation Framework

Goal: Prevent low-birth-weight babies

Evaluation Plan: Assess nutrition change of participants via pre- and post-self-report

Objective: Improve prenatal nutrition by 20% by June 30, 20xx

Implementation Plan: 12-week workshop for pregnant women and their partners on nutrition

FOUR STEPS TO PREPARING THE OBJECTIVES AND EVALUATION PLAN

Step 1: State the Expected Outcomes or Results

We look at the program goal, which in this case is to eliminate obesity in college-age youth, and then we itemize the program components you plan to address that contribute to causing obesity in college-age youth. The components we want to work with are 1) poor nutrition, 2) lack of exercise, 3) depression, 4) lack of access to healthy foods.

First Objective: Improve the nutritional intake of 200 college-age students by 25% by June 30, 20xx.

- It provides the number and type of participants. Check.

- It specifies what is expected to happen with the students. Check.

- It provides a timeline of the service. Check

Second Objective: 80 self-identified, sedentary college-age students will increase their activity by 25% by June 30, 20xx.

- Meets the criteria above? Check.

Third Objective: 20 students with depression will increase their knowledge about the causes and cures for depression by 20% by June 29, 20xx.

- Meets the measurable criteria above? Check.

Sometimes so-called proxy outcomes are developed. For example, you may wish to improve birth outcomes by decreasing the incidence of low-birth-weight babies. However, this may be difficult to measure. At the same time, research has shown that there is a direct link between women receiving early prenatal care and improved birth outcomes. Therefore, one can use getting women into early prenatal care as a proxy measure for the desired outcome of improved birth weight.

In many cases, the program will not only achieve short- and long-term outcomes for the participants but may also have a long-term impact on the community or society at large. For example, the cumulative effect of women participating in this prenatal program may also lead to an overall improvement in the county's health care indicators. Such a long-term evaluation can be a costly evaluation design, and so it is rarely completed. We use short-term measures to view change in the steps toward the goal.

The beginning grant writer is apt to confuse an objective with an implementation activity. A common error is to write the actual program or service that is going to be offered without indicating its benefits. Such an error would result in the following example of a *poor* objective:

One thousand youths between the ages of 12 and 16 will participate in a 6-week education program on violence prevention by June 30, 20xx.

In this example, the "6-week education program" is an implementation activity and does not describe what the impact will be on the participants regarding violence prevention. The following questions may help the writer reach the outcome level of the objective: Why are youths receiving a 6-week program? To increase their knowledge or improve their skills? To change behavior? A revised, well-stated objective would look like this:

One thousand youths between the ages of 12 and 16 will increase their knowledge by 40% in conflict resolution and anger management by June 30, 20xx.

Depending on the length of the program or service and the nature of the intervention, changes may occur at different rates. It may be easier to increase one's *knowledge* about a subject (short-term outcome) but take longer to *change behavior* (intermediate or long-term outcome).

Examples include the following:

- Increase knowledge about healthy foods (short term)

- Reduce body mass index (intermediate or long term)

As you write your objectives, make sure you are stating the expected *outcome* or changes in the program recipients and not just identifying the approach being used. In summary, the following example shows how a single goal can lead to several process and outcome objectives:

<u>**Sample Goal 1:**</u> To prevent drug use among young people by promoting their academic success and emotional well-being

Sample Process Objective 1:
To form a coalition of 10 youth-serving agencies to develop a comprehensive plan for providing after-school activities at two junior high schools by June 30, 20xx

Sample Outcome Objective 1:
One hundred at-risk junior high school students will increase their knowledge by 60% about the dangers of drug and alcohol use by June 30, 20xx.

Sample Outcome Objective 2:
One hundred junior high school students who are academically at risk will show a 30% improvement in their reading and math scores by June 30, 20xx.

Sample Outcome Objective 3:
One hundred parents will increase their knowledge by 40% in effective communication techniques for teaching their children about decision-making, goal setting, and the dangers of drugs by June 30, 20xx.

It could be summarized that the *goal statement* provides a general aim and direction for the project but lacks in specificity as to what will be achieved. Process objectives identify the approach to be used but do not state what impact it will have on the participants. (It is not necessary for every proposal to have both process and outcome objectives. *Process objectives* are written when the funder has indicated that the desired outcome is to develop a new approach or test out a particular method of service delivery.) And finally, *outcome objectives* specify "who" and "how many" are to achieve "what results" by "when."

Common errors in writing objectives include: 1) putting more than one measurable outcome in the objective and 2) saying much more than is needed in the objective. Keep the objectives simple and clear. Although you want to "stretch" as far as possible with a vision for improved conditions or circumstances, objectives should be realistic and not promise more than can be delivered within the time period stated. In most cases, it is the objectives that are directly tied to the contractual relationship between the agency and the funder, and as such, the agency may be held accountable to meet the objective.

Step Two: Determine the Type of Evidence Needed

Now let's look at the kinds of things we can measure so we can develop a measurable outcome object for each component. We want to know if the outcome happened as projected in the objective. To determine this, we need to know how to measure change. The usual change indicators are known as KABS:

- Knowledge—What does the individual know about this issue, and can increasing their knowledge affect the way the person relates to the issue? Can knowledge prevent problems?

- Attitudes—How does a person feel in relation to the problem? Does their belief set contribute to their participation in the problem? Is their belief set harmful to themselves? Can it be changed?

- Behavior—How does the person act? Do they say one thing but do another? Impacting behavior is considered to be high-level change; however, people can say they will, but until they incorporate that change into behavior, it is all talk.

- Skills—Does the person want to change but lacks the skill set to accomplish this? For example, they are emotionally ready to work but don't have a driver's license, or they can't read? Skill development would lead to improved outcomes for this client.

The easiest type of indicator measure is knowledge change because you can give a pretest before the intervention to determine the amount of knowledge a person currently has, then give a posttest to determine the amount of knowledge the person has at the end of the service, and calculate the difference. (Here is a simple formula to determine percentage of change: *1) subtract the old value from the new value, 2) divide that number by the old value, and 3) multiply by 100 to convert that rate to a percentage. Example: A student score on the pretest was 82 points and 92 points on the posttest. 92 – 82 = 10. 10/82 = 0.1219 x 100 = 12.19% or simply 12%.*)

It is often more difficult to determine change when it comes to behavior. In most cases, the evaluation plan will take a self-report from the participant to determine current levels and then another self-report at the end of the intervention or treatment to determine change. Another way to measure behavioral change is to observe the client in the new behaviors.

This leads us to another issue: sample size. The usual rule of thumb is to sample 10% of the group up to a group size of 1,000. Or, another way to determine sample size is to use the Krejcie and Morgan Sample Size Table (in Appendix D), which provides you with greater accuracy. You can select your method based on what degree of precision you need in your sampling. (There are many websites to assist in evaluation issues—one such good site has been put together in Kenya by young professionals at www.kenpro.org.)

As you develop the evaluation design, be aware of the tendency to overpromise outcomes and to use large sample sizes. People will normally drop out of programs, and some people will not change as much as others. You want to strike a balance between providing the most robust evaluation you can and overpromising.

As you can see, determining the appropriate measures that represent the expected results takes time and a thorough understanding of the changes your approach will yield. In recent years, there have been compilations of indicators typically used in human services programming, and much of the program evaluation data can now be found on funder's websites. For example, you can visit Centers for Disease Control and Prevention, review studies that have been conducted on obesity, and see the indicators and measures they used. Table 7.1 provides examples of common indicators.

Step 3: Determine the Data Collection Plan

The next step is to identify the evidence that represents the achievement of the outcome objectives. There are usually two parts to this: first, did the number of participants stated in the objective actually participate? How can a project count this? Did the activity actually take place? The ways in which this data can be collected include the following:

TABLE 7.1 ● Common Indicators

Healthy Births

- Increased knowledge about prenatal care

- Lower rates of low-birth-weight babies

- Higher rates of prenatal care in the first trimester

- Early prenatal care

Substance Abuse

- Increased knowledge about the dangers of alcohol and drug use

- Percent of youth in grades 7–12 who consume less than five or more drinks of alcohol on a single occasion in the last 30 days

- Duration of abstinence

- Number of relapse events

Parent Functioning

- Improved scores on parenting skills

- Increased time spent reading to children

- Employing nonviolent techniques of discipline

- Decreased parental stress and family violence

Education

- Dropout rates by district

- Percentage of third graders who read

- Standardized test results

- Report cards

Mental Health

- Depression and anxiety indicators

- Stress measures

- Overall functioning and quality of life indicators

- Participant sign-up and sign-in sheets (which are most useful if you have to prove that an individual actually participated in a class or activity)

- Agenda and minutes of meetings

- Visitor logs

- Written requests for products or services

- Participant interviews

- Movies or photos of the event and participants

- Staff schedules, calendars, or phone logs

- Newspaper articles about the activity

- Direct counts

The second part is to measure the change. The ways in which this data can be collected include the following:

- Pre- and posttesting of client knowledge

- Assessment or survey of attitudes, values, and beliefs

- Observation

- Individual interview

- Focus groups (a form of interviewing in a group)

(There are a variety of publications to help you find tests that can measure family functioning, self-esteem, coping skills, cognitive functioning, anxiety, depression, aggression, anger, eating, activity, etc. Many of these can be administered by anyone [some have restricted use to licensed professionals]. You can start a search at Mental Measurements Yearbook, Tests in Print, or Standardized Tests and Measure to name a few.)

Table 7.2 summarizes components of a data collection plan.

Step 4: Identify Data Analysis and Reporting Procedures

Now that we know what we want to measure as an outcome, we need a data collection plan. Let's consider the following:

1. Identify the person(s) in the project who will be responsible for developing or selecting the data collection tools.

2. Consider when the data will be collected—at entry, at first service, at midpoint, at the end, or in follow-up?

3. Will the evaluation design require there to be any comparison or control group(s)? These would be comparable people who don't receive the service.

4. Are the tools likely to meet the needs of the cultures involved, or will there be a need to find specific cultural appropriate measures?

5. Will the evaluation require human subject protections including assuring voluntary participation in the evaluation, proper treatment protocols,

TABLE 7.2 ⬡ Components of a Data Collection Plan			
Method	**Data Sources**	**Data Collection Methods**	**Evaluation Focus**
Questionnaire or Survey	Stakeholders Program staff Community members	Face-to-face Mail Phone Internet	Needs assessment Process evaluation Output evaluation Short-/mid-/long-term outcome evaluation
Interview	Key informants Participants	Face-to-face Phone Internet	Needs assessment Output evaluation Outcome evaluation
Focus Group	Participants Service providers	Face-to-face Internet	Needs assessment Output evaluation Outcome evaluation Program contribution analysis
Observation	Behavior observation records Service provider field notes	Field trip	Needs assessment Process evaluation Outcome evaluation
Database	Public/state/local records	Secondary data	Needs assessment Impact evaluation
Program Records	Sign-in sheets Attendance records Service logs	Generated through program activities	Process evaluation Output evaluation

and protection of client confidentiality, and so on? Who in the project is responsible to ensure this is completed?

6. Select sampling plans, including type of sample, and size (if applicable, see Sample Size table in Appendix D).

The federal government has developed a data collection protocol known as GPRA (pronounced gip-rah). This is short for the Government Performance and Results Act law enacted in 1993 to improve government accountability. Basically, the law requires that all contractors with the federal government meet the criteria established by the law and comply with data collection protocols submitted to the Office of Budget Management each year. The GPRA requirements will be stated in the proposal application packet. (The GPRA mandate is in Appendix D.)

Evaluation data are usually presented to the funder on either a quarterly or semiannual basis and at the project's end. Project data should be presented in a graphically rich format—using charts and graphs to illustrate the outcomes.

A LOGIC MODEL

The program components you have developed can now be incorporated into a *logic model* (see Appendix F for a template), which according to Knowlton and Phillips (2009), includes the following:

> a visual method of presenting an idea. They offer a way to describe and share an understanding of relationships among elements necessary to operate a program or change effort. Logic models describe a bounded project or initiative: both what is planned (the doing) and what results are expected (the getting). They provide a clear roadmap to a specified end. (p. 5)

The logic model presents a snapshot of the program and its core components. It consists of *inputs* (the resources that will be used to implement a project), *activities* (processes that will use the resources to deliver services to the community), *outputs* (countable products of activities), *short-, mid-,* and *long-term outcomes* (measurable changes and results that the project aims to achieve to address a community need), and impact (long-term change that is the main focus of the program but is usually beyond the immediate scope and timeline of the project). The logic of the model is tested by verifying that the inputs support activities, activities produce outputs, outputs lead to outcomes, and outcomes result in long-term impact for the communities.

Table 7.3 presents a logic model format with expected content. (Funders may have different format expectations.)

WRITING THE EVALUATION SECTION

Program evaluation may be presented in a narrative form, in an outline, or on a funder-developed form (we will use a Scope of Work form in the next section). If no specific instructions have been given for preparing this section, the following is a typical format:

Inputs– Resources	Process– Activities	Outputs– Measurements	Outcomes– Changes/ Benefits (Short, Intermediate, or Long Term)	Impact on the Community (Long Term)
Human Resources	• Education	• Number of persons who attend	• Increased number of healthy meals eaten each week	Improved community health indicators:
• Staff	• Training			
• Volunteers	• Counseling	• Number of persons who complete	• Reduced body mass index	• Reduced diabetes
• Consultants	• Health Care activities			
• Clients	• Evaluation and assessment	• Number of hours associated with services and activities	• Lowered blood pressure	• Reduced heart disease
			• Elevated mood and reduced depression	• Reduced sick time away from work
Material Resources		• Client logs or sign-in sheets		
• Facility				
• Travel		• Pre- and posttests, physical exams, or other observational measures		
• Communications				
• Project materials		• Materials produced		
• Technology		• Participant feedback about services		

TABLE 7.3 ⬢ Sample Logic Model

Outline for an Evaluation Plan

  I. Identify the Evaluation Goals

 II. Describe the Evaluation Design

III. Identify What Will Be Measured

 IV. Describe the Data Collection Plan

   A. The Indicators or Type of Data

   B. Source of the Data

   C. Data Collection Procedures

   D. Timetable

  V. Describe Sampling Plan (if applicable)

 VI. Discuss Data Analysis Techniques

    VII. Address Protection of Human Subjects and Cultural Relevancy

   VIII. Explain Staffing and Management Plans for the Evaluation

    IX. Identify Reporting Procedures

     X. Show Proposed Budget

ETHICAL CONSIDERATIONS

If you are designing a program evaluation that requests individuals share their feelings, beliefs, or other personal data beyond simple likes or dislikes, it is appropriate to ask for the consent of the individual through the use of an *informed consent* form. (Obtain consent from a parent or guardian if your client is a minor.) This consent form would itemize those things that are being requested in the evaluation such as personal data, health status including drug and alcohol history, HIV status, and so on, and then you would list any possible risk to the individual such as psychological distress at recalling events. You would provide access to counseling if need be and someone to talk to if they have any other questions. Most of the evaluation that you will conduct in human service and educational settings will be exempt from human subject review regulations. If the evaluation has the potential to harm an individual, such as research in clinical trials and biomedical research, then it would be necessary to obtain approval for this research by application to an institutional review board (IRB) or ethical review board (ERB). Most universities have such a review board. (See Appendix D for the text of the Code of Federal Regulations that discusses who is exempt from these regulations.)

Keep your evaluation data under lock and key, and have a plan to allow only authorized persons access to confidential information on clients. You must also protect client information from view of other clients, so even as you collect data, ensure that it is handled in such a way as to maintain client confidentiality.

It is also important to consider cultural factors when developing your data collection strategies. Factors such as attitudes toward outsiders, the interpretation of the meaning of words, and mistrust or suspicion of how data will be used can affect your ability to collect the data as well as the reliability of your results. If you are designing an evaluation on an ethnic group you are not familiar with, obtain consultation or research on appropriate measures and implementation.

KEY POINTS FOR CHAPTER 7

1. Project evaluation can focus on processes and outcomes; the latter is most common for grants and is frequently required by sponsors.

2. An evaluation plan includes expected outcomes, a description of the evidence needed, a data collection plan, and data analysis methods.

3. A logic model is a useful, visual way of presenting the components of a program (i.e., its inputs, activities, outputs, outcomes, and impact) and helps the reader understand the program at a glance.

CHAPTER 7 ACTIVITY

Chapter 7 Activity 1

Start drafting a logic model for your project.

Share your work with someone and explain your ideas.

WRITING THE NEED OR PROBLEM STATEMENT

THE AIM OF THE NEED/PROBLEM STATEMENT

This chapter begins the *writing* sections of the book. As we said, we are prepping you to write a state or federal proposal complete with *Scope of Work* forms. Once you prepare a proposal in this structure, you will be able to prepare any proposal. The first part of the Request for Proposals (RFP) will ask you to submit a need statement or problem statement (or statement of need) that describes the problem and provides the rationale for the request for funding. It is often limited to three or so pages, and it demands that you craft a succinct statement using data and other objective measures to demonstrate and substantiate the need for providing resources to address the concern.

The term *need statement* is generally used in seeking funding for programs or services, while *problem statement* usually applies to research-oriented proposals. In some professions, however, a *need* refers to the lack of access to something that is deemed desirable or fundamental to an individual or community's well-being (e.g., jobs, health care, child care). In contrast, a *problem* refers to difficulty, trouble, or negative behavior and outcomes (e.g., drug abuse, child abuse, domestic violence).

Oftentimes, the terms are used interchangeably. For our purposes, we will use the more common *need statement* because our primary focus is on proposals written to improve conditions or address a problem existing within your community.

This section of your proposal does *not* describe your approach to address the need or problem; rather, it provides a strong *rationale for why* support should be provided. The need statement is rooted in data and other factual information to understand the problem not only at the level at which you provide services but also within the larger context of the community, state, or nation. Consider the following two examples, both seeking to offer a high school equivalency program in the community:

> There are 1,000 individuals in Agency X's service area without a high school diploma, which limits their ability to meet the labor market needs in the area.

> versus

> X County has one of the lowest high school completion rates in the state ranking in the lowest third of in the nation. The unemployment rate in X County of 11.4% is double the national rate. More than 1,000 individuals, or nearly 60% of the residents, ages 18–35, in the county are without a high school diploma or a job while entry-level jobs go unfilled (82% of local businesses require a high school diploma).

Although the first example provided accurate information about the concerns in the service area, the second placed the needs of the service area in a broader context of the county and the nation. Thus, the funder can feel that supporting this project has a "rolling effect" by not only benefitting the community but also improving the conditions within the county, the state, and ultimately, the nation.

An effective need statement does five things:

1. Uses supportive evidence to clearly describe the nature and extent of the need/problem facing those you plan to serve

2. Places the nature and extent of the need/problem in a broader context than the immediate environment or setting

3. Illuminates the factors contributing to the problem or the circumstances creating the need

4. Identifies current gaps in services or programs

5. Provides a rationale for the transferability of the promising approaches or best practices to the population you seek to serve

The need statement makes clear what is occurring that requires prompt attention before conditions worsen, provides an explanation as to why the problem or need exists, and identifies some of the strategies used in other settings, such as *evidence-based practices* that have the potential for addressing the problem or need in your area. You must thoroughly understand the significance of the need/problem section because it provides the underpinnings of the remainder of the proposal. As stated before, this section is not the place in the proposal to propose your particular solution or project. Rather, it lays the foundation for your particular solution to emerge as one that is responsive to the need.

The need statement provides an understanding of the impact of the problem not only on those directly affected but also on others, including the community and/or the state and nation as a whole. A compelling case should be made as to what effect continued *non-intervention* may have on individuals, families, and the community at large. One way to make this case is to contrast the costs of prevention or timely intervention to ongoing costs of not addressing the problem (e.g., effective outcomes-based diversion programs versus incarceration). In addition, there are emotional and psychological costs to consider related to quality of life issues for the program participants and for the community (e.g., impact of being in an abusive home environment on a child's school behavior and learning).

Ideally, the need statement is comprehensive in its treatment of the problem but not boring. Be judicious in your selection of data, and use that which most pointedly tells the story of those you intend to serve. As you write the need section you want to accomplish the following:

•   demonstrate that you have a thorough understanding of the need or problem and those you seek to serve;

•   demonstrate that you are knowledgeable of the types of interventions that are successful in addressing this need or problem for your client base;

•   indicate that you are aware of the multitude of barriers that may hamper the provision of service to this population;

•   demonstrate that it is the same issue that the funder wants to address; and

•   lay the groundwork to lead the funder to the conclusion that your approach is client centered or community focused and, ultimately, is one of the best possible choices to address this problem.

A GUIDE TO WRITING THE NEED STATEMENT

Obviously, you cannot use all of the data you find. Scrutinize it carefully to make the best possible case for your proposal. At this point in the process, many grant writers face the mounds of data in front of them with increasing anxiety. The problem now becomes one of condensing and editing the data to make a powerful statement within a limited number of pages.

The following sections provide a template to help you organize your thinking. This is not meant to be your final version of the document, nor is this meant to be used as a verbatim method of presentation. We are using hypothetical data for illustrative purposes and creating a scaffolding for you to begin to organize your thoughts. Of course, you will need to use your own data and create your own compelling statement, but this will help get you started.

Section One: The Nature and Extent of the Need/Problem

This section could be subtitled, "What is the problem and who is experiencing it?" In it, you will try to provide a clear picture of the incidence of the problem (e.g., the number of people per thousand in the population who experience the problem and the rates by ethnicity, gender, age, and educational level or other pertinent demographics).

In this example, we begin with a factual opening sentence that states the topic and captures the attention of the reader. We begin to define the problem and give a percent of the total population who experiences homelessness in the geographical area to be served.

> The majority of families are only one paycheck away from homelessness and for (*# of people*) in (*your local geographic area*), this fact is all too real. The majority of homeless (defined as those without semi-permanent or permanent shelter) in (*your county*) are single mothers with children, representing the fastest-growing segment of the homeless population.

The next step is to compare the local-level data to the state and national data. If the incidence of the problem is greater than the state or national rates, your job is easy, and your next sentence might sound like this:

> In fact, in (*year*) a total of ____ persons were homeless. The homelessness rate in (*your county*) was ____, which exceeded the state rate of ____ and the national rate of ____ in the same year (*source of data*).

If your rate is lower than the state and national rates, study the data and see if there is a significant change in the rate in your own county from the past, and you may be able to say something like this:

> Although lower than the state and national rates of ____ and ____, respectively, (*your county*) has seen a significant increase in homelessness over the past 5 years and, without intervention, will meet and exceed national rates within the next ____ years (*source of data*).

If your rate is so low as to make your application noncompetitive, you may need to find some other unique reason as to why your community's problem is significant. For example, you may have higher crime rates than surrounding counties or more health problems within the homeless population.

In this next paragraph, we want to know who is homeless in your county. What is their ethnicity? What is their educational background? Are they single persons or a family? Are they young or old?

> In (*your county*), the rate of homelessness by ethnicity is ____% white, ____% Latino, ____% Black, and ____% Asian. The rate for (*ethnic group*) is proportionately higher than all others.

> The average educational level for the homeless population is 10 years of schooling. The majority of homeless in our county are single Black men (40%), followed by white men and women (30%), followed by white and Black families (20%), and 10% Asian men and women.

You will notice that we have not made a highly emotional appeal to the funder but have already put a face on the client in the first paragraph. We feel that the funder, as well as the human service provider, is all too aware of the personal toll these problems bring. Overdramatizing the problem can work to your disadvantage.

In the preceding example, the data are effectively presented within the context of the community. When you place data in relationship to other data (e.g., state or national level), or other associated problems, you strengthen your request and increase the sense of urgency. For example, compare the following two statements:

> Fifty percent of the young people in the county do not graduate from high school.

> versus

> Fifty percent of the young people in the county do not graduate from high school compared to a 10% dropout rate in the state and 27% in the nation.

Section Two: Factors Contributing to the Problem or Conditions

In this section of the proposal, you will address the causes of the problem and the needs of the clients, which may stem from a variety of factors such as these:

1. a lack of skill, knowledge, or awareness;

2. debilitating attitudes or harmful values;

3. physical or mental challenges and limitations;

4. dysfunctional or problem behavior;

5. limited resources or access to services;

6. institutional and systemic barriers including fragmented services; and

7. policies, practices, or laws that have negative consequences (either intended or unintended).

You want to account for each of the factors that cause the problem you are addressing. The following paragraph is a beginning to that end:

> There are a variety of conditions that may ultimately lead to homelessness. Of the homeless population, ____% have severe and persistent mental illness; ____% have experienced the loss of a job; ____% have recently divorced; and ____% have been incarcerated ____ (*source of data, year*).
>
> The top reason for job loss in the past year was personal health problems, including depression, followed by poor work performance, a lack of job-related skills, absenteeism, and health problems with other family members. In most cases, homelessness does not happen all at once. The family utilizes all available resources to maintain housing and often have 1 to 3 months of financial struggle before ending up on the streets.

It is also likely that a discussion of barriers to addressing this problem will be included in this section. For example, the stigma associated with homelessness may be so great as to cause people to delay seeking assistance, or the clients themselves may have attitudes or beliefs that prevent them from benefiting from assistance.

Each of these causes of the problem as stated in the preceding example is significant to program planning with different or complementary approaches and can be further developed along socioeconomic and cultural lines, if need be. The second paragraph, which indicates that homelessness "evolves," is laying some of the groundwork necessary to support our project—early intervention to help shore up individuals to prevent impending homelessness—but of course, we will not say anything about this in this section.

Circular Reasoning

Finally, we want to warn you about one of the most common mistakes we see in this section of the proposal, which is known as *circular reasoning* (Kiritz, 1980). Circular reasoning occurs when one argues that the problem is the lack of service that one is proposing. For example, you may write in the need statement:

> The problem facing many teens is that they do not have access to a teen peer support group.

After writing this, you may proceed merrily on your way to proposing teen support groups in solution to the problem. This statement, however, has failed to identify the needs teens have that can be met through a peer support group (e.g., loneliness, isolation, depression, etc.) and, in fact, gives the idea that the absence of a teen support group is the problem! Consider the way in which the following example might better address the needs:

> An adolescent spends an average of _____ hours per day in contact with other teens in school and after-school activities. Research indicates that teens obtain approximately _____% of their information on drugs, sexuality, and health-related topics from their peers (*source of data, year*). From a developmental perspective, teens are moving away from parental and other adult authority and into the development of their own personal authority. In this process, teens attach to and relate best to their peers.

Thus, you have laid the groundwork for understanding the importance of a teen peer support program in addressing the developmental needs of this age group.

Section Three: Impact of the Problem

In this section, you want to look at the impact the problem has on the individual, the person's family, and the community at large and the benefits to be derived through intervention, treatment, or prevention of the problem. The following paragraphs begin this process:

> The problem of homelessness exacts a significant toll on the homeless person and family. Children who are homeless are often uprooted from their schools and their friends, suffer from poor nutrition, and lack even the most basic of preventive care services (e.g., immunizations). For example, 65% of school-age homeless children are without immunizations. If one is a homeless adult, one has no address or phone number to use to obtain employment.

> Once an individual is homeless, the demands on community resources are great. The Government Accounting Office has estimated that it costs taxpayers approximately $35,000 per homeless family per year to provide for basic needs. In a study by _____, it was shown that timely intervention targeted at a family in crisis costs approximately $15,000 per year, a savings of more than half of the cost of delayed intervention! In addition to the significant financial savings, homeless children suffered fewer days lost from school and experienced improved health outcomes.

As you might have guessed, we continue to lay the groundwork for our early intervention project in response to the problem of homelessness. We want to show that our proposed project is cost-effective and reduces the negative consequences associated with homelessness. *But* we won't say anything about the proposed project in this section either.

Section Four: Promising Approaches for Improved Results

In this section, you can discuss the theoretical perspectives that have proven to be useful in designing interventions, successful approaches used in other geographic areas, and more than likely, you will discuss the barriers to improving the problem.

> Several promising strategies have been developed to address the problem of homelessness. The first is the Homeless Project based in Seattle, Washington. This project targeted a subset of homeless drug-abusing adults using the psychosocial rehabilitation approach, treatment incentives, and

comprehensive services. The program helped greater than 67% of its participants kick the drug habit, and after a year, 87% of those were employed and paying for their own housing.

Other projects have been extremely successful in helping individuals in crisis avoid homelessness altogether. One project, in Michigan, opened a one-stop service center for struggling families. Through a combination of debt counseling, psychological services, educational remediation, job training, and health services, a full 90% of clients maintained their homes. In addition, this approach has the advantage of avoiding public resistance to a homeless shelter in the community.

You are referencing the particular theoretical and practical program components that will be effective in addressing the need/problem. This means you will demonstrate an understanding of the applicability of others' efforts in addressing the same or similar problem/need in your area. For example, psychosocial rehabilitation is named as a theoretical orientation and service component. It would be useful to briefly describe this approach, giving the success rate, treatment advantages, and cost-effectiveness both at your agency and other agencies. Discuss the pros and cons of particular strategies, and consider the unique needs (e.g., cultural, gender, sexual orientation, age, income, or educational level, etc.) of your participants.

THEORY OF CHANGE

We feel it is important to discuss the concept of a *theory of change* because some funders may request that you state your theory of change in relation to the project you are proposing. An organization called GrantCraft (n.d.) outlines the difference between a logic model and theory of change:

> A theory of change takes a wide view of a desired change, carefully probing the assumptions behind each step in what may be a long and complex process. Articulating a theory of change often entails thinking through all the steps along a path toward a desired change, identifying the preconditions that will enable (and possibly inhibit) each step, listing the activities that will produce those conditions, and explaining why those activities are likely to work. It is often, but not always, presented as a flow chart.

> A logic model takes a more narrowly practical look at the relationship between inputs and results. It is often presented as a table listing the steps from inputs or resources through the achievement of a desired program

goal. Some grant makers use separate logic models to chart the implementation components of theory of change.

(You are welcome to excerpt, copy, or quote from GrantCraft materials, with attribution to GrantCraft and inclusion of the copyright. © 2006 GrantCraft.)

When a funder asks you for your theory of change, Figure 8.1 outlines what is expected.

If you are working for a nonprofit, it is likely that the agency has developed a theory of change in relation to the problems it seeks to address within the local community. For example, another excerpt from GrantCraft (n.d.) states:

> Another grant maker explained the theory behind a program to improve conditions for low-income children: "The basic idea was that children do well when their families do well, and families do well when they're supported in neighborhoods, and being a supportive neighborhood means having opportunities for families to connect to economic opportunity, social networks, and quality services and supports. . . . It was a different way to frame the problem. The problem isn't families; the problem is that families aren't connected." That insight led the foundation's program staff to ask local teams of residents to design interventions to help families connect to systems of support in their own neighborhoods.

FIGURE 8.1 ● Theory of Change

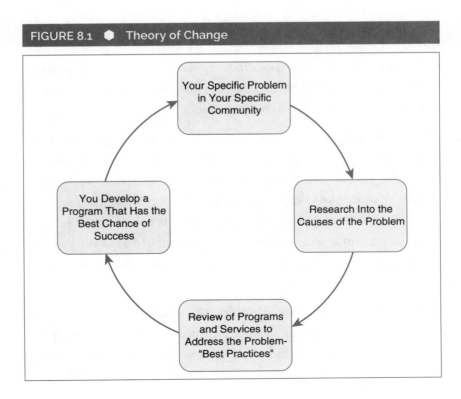

When developing a theory of change for the program, it is useful to think about three main components: 1) the context (structures and culture) that exist regardless of the program and that will serve as the foundation for the program you plan to propose; 2) the mechanisms (resources the program plans to bring in and reactions of the program participants) that will be used to initiate and support change; and 3) the outcomes that the program wants to achieve within the existing context by activating the mechanisms of change. Context-mechanism-outcome links are the building blocks of the change theory that you can use in describing your proposal.

KEY POINTS FOR CHAPTER 8

1. The need statement focuses on the conditions and problems that exist in a community, but it does not yet describe the approach that will be used to address it.

2. The need statement describes the nature of the problem, factors that contribute to the problem, impact, and promising approaches for improved results.

CHAPTER 8 ACTIVITIES

Chapter 8 Activity 1

Formulate a problem that you would like to address through a funded project. Answer the questions that follow to start developing your need statement.

- What data supports that the problem exists?

- What factors contribute to the problem?

- What impact does this problem have on the community?

- Who is affected? What challenges do they experience?

- What approaches can be used to solve the problem? Which is the best/optimal approach and why?

Chapter 8 Activity 2

Write a two-paragraph need statement, and share it with someone. Ask them to highlight all sections that are hard to read. Next, ask them to underline the sections that seem out of place or irrelevant to the main argument for the need in a community.

What alternative approaches can you use to describe the existing problem and need?

9

PROGRAM DESCRIPTION

The program description portion of many state and federal applications represents a section containing the 1) logic model, 2) project narrative (this section includes the goals and objectives, implementation activities, timeline, and evaluation). We also present Scope of Work forms in this section.

IMPLEMENTATION PLAN

The *implementation plan* provides a clear account of what you plan to do, who will do it, and in what time frame the activities will be accomplished. Although we introduced this section to you in Chapter 6, we will provide you with additional examples to help you think this section through. The discussion of the implementation plan will be organized into three parts: 1) preparatory activities or inputs-resources, 2) process or specific program-related activities, and 3) units of service.

Preparatory Activities (Also Known as Inputs)

Regardless of the type of program you wish to undertake, there are a common set of activities that usually are considered at the beginning of the project. We refer to these as *preparatory activities*, that is, the start-up activities or general tasks necessary to get the program underway. (Funders usually assume that you have space to house the program you are developing. If this is not the case and you need project time to locate and secure a facility, you should include that in the preparatory activities.) With each task, it is also useful to identify the person responsible for accomplishing the activity and to estimate the time needed for completion (this will make it easier to complete a timeline). Although the type of preparatory activities will vary depending upon the nature of your program, Table 9.1 lists typical activities.

Process- or Specific Program-Related Activities

The format for an implementation activity is generally: who is responsible, what is to be done and by when, and how will it be evaluated. The following service topic listing itemizes some of the main activities that should be considered:

Training and Education

Examples: Community Educational Programs, School-Based Programs, or Training-the-Trainer Programs

1. What is the content of the presentation(s)?

2. Who will conduct the training? What criteria will be used to select and supervise trainers?

TABLE 9.1 ● Preparatory Activities		
Activity	**Responsible Person**	**Time Needed**
Recruit and Hire Staff and Volunteers	Executive Director/Project Director	First 2 Months
Site/Facilities and Communications	Executive Director/Project Director	First Month
Order Special Equipment	Project Director	First Month
Obtain Program Materials	Project Director	First 2 Months
Secure Interagency Agreements	Executive Director/Project Director	First Month
Conduct Client Outreach	Project Director	First 2 Months
Create Program Forms Such as HIPAA and Sign-in Sheets	Project Director	First Month
Establish Accounting and Reporting Processes	Executive Director/Project Director	First Month
Develop Staff and Volunteer Schedules	Project Director	First Month
Set Evaluation Mechanisms	Project Director	First Month

3. How will participants be recruited? How will they give consent?

4. What will be the typical format and schedule? Does it take into consideration the program participants' needs and schedule?

5. How will the services be evaluated? Will it require a special evaluation team?

Information Development and Dissemination

Examples: Ad Campaign for Drug Abuse Prevention, Videotape on AIDS Prevention, Health Care Newsletter, Parent Training Manual, Resource and Referral Service

1. Who is the targeted audience?

2. What is the content and format?

3. How will it be developed? Who will develop it?

4. Which group(s) will review before distribution to determine effectiveness and appropriateness?

5. What dissemination strategies will be utilized?

Counseling, Self-Efficacy, and Other Support Services

Examples: Bereavement Counseling, Support Group for Victims of Abuse and Violence, Drug and Alcohol Abuse Counseling, and Crisis Hotline

1. What counseling strategies or techniques will be used?

2. What are the underlying assumptions or evidence of the validity of the techniques with the specific population?

3. What will be the counseling process and format?

4. What issues and content will be addressed?

5. What others resources (e.g., support system, professionals) will be needed by the program participants?

6. What are the plans to reduce the attrition rate?

Provision of Resources or Changing Conditions

Examples: Transportation for the Disabled, Meals Program for Older Americans, Youth Recreation Program, Health Care Screening

1. What resources will be provided?

2. What is the most effective delivery approach for the population?

3. When, where, and how will they be delivered?

4. Who will develop, organize, and deliver them?

5. Any special equipment and/or materials needed? How will these be obtained?

Revenue-Generating Activities

Examples: Program Services and Sales, for example, Local Bakery, Computer Training Courses, Low-Cost Medical Services

1. What services will be provided during the program?

2. What fees are currently charged or will be collected?

3. Who, where, and how will collect service fees?

4. How will sales and service fees be reinvested in the program?

5. How do services and sales support the overall mission and goals of the program?

Units of Service (Also Known as Outputs)

In addition to identifying the tasks to be undertaken, one must also provide *how much* of that activity will be provided. Often referred to as the *output* of your program, this question relates to the volume of work that is expected or the products of your program. It describes the types or amounts of service provided. Examples include: 100 hours of group counseling with 75 drug abuse addicts for a total of 7,500 units of service or 150 high school dropouts attending 10 hours of computer training sessions for a total of 1,500 units of service.

The results or outcomes are influenced by how well the program has been conceptualized and whether there were sufficient units of service to achieve the objective. It is helpful to apply a simple cost/benefit calculation. Divide the cost of the service by the units of service to see what one unit of service costs. If, for example, you find a unit of service costs very little, you should probably add more units or add types of service under this cost center. If you find that the cost of this unit is sky high, you may need to change the service. For example, if a person can have a session with a counselor at a nonprofit agency for $50 and your cost per session worked out to be $500, it is unlikely to be funded.

THE PROJECT NARRATIVE

This section may also be referred to in the proposal guidelines as the *program narrative*. It brings together your conceptualization of the work plan including the preparatory and program-related activities. Included within this section are subsections sometimes referred to as the *Scope of Work*, the *methods section*, or *program approach*. (If proposal instructions lack specific details about how to write this section, begin with the goal(s) of the project, followed by the objective, the implementation activities, and a detailed description of the evaluation method.) This section allows you to bring more detail into the narrative including the rationale for particular program and staffing levels, for example, than in any other section of the proposal. The project narrative describes planned activities in detail sufficient for the reviews to get a clear picture of what, when, how, and by whom will be done. The description of the program approach is frequently organized around the project objectives. Refer to Chapter 7 to review the types of objectives and best practices for outlining them. The following is an example of a *project narrative*:

> The Learning for Life Project has two goals. The first is to ensure that all children receive a quality education and the second is to eliminate school dropouts. The first objective under goal one states:
>
> **Objective** 1.1: Fifty percent (50%) of two hundred (200) low-income school-age children in the XYZ School District will improve their grade level by one full level by June 30, 20xx.
>
> Implementation Activities:
>
> Children will be selected into the program based on their eligibility for federally funded lunch programs at the schools and invited to participate in the project through 1) a personal invitation to the student from the teacher, 2) a personal note to the parent(s) from the teacher, and 3) a formal letter sent to parents from the agency describing the project and obtaining consent. In-kind donations will give school supplies to participating students, and parents will receive a voucher for school clothes and groceries. Approximately three cohorts of 70 students each will be enrolled into the program three times over the year.
>
> The project director will interview and test each of the 200 children in the first 3 months of the project. The results of the testing will be used

to match the child with the learning specialist (on staff) and a tutor (the tutors will be hired to start services by month three).

Each child will receive 10 hours of targeted tutoring each week for 10 weeks. At the end of 10 weeks, each student will be retested to determine any change in grade level. If 100 students have increased their grade level by one full level, the objective will be met. The project director will be responsible to oversee the evaluation component.

You will continue to describe the project in this narrative format, and you may also be asked to use a Scope of Work form. This may seem redundant to you, and it is.

PROJECT TIMELINE

In addition to describing the project activities, funders typically desire to see a schedule of those activities. A visual display of the action plan provides the reader with a real sense of when different phases of the project will be undertaken. It also helps generate confidence in your ability to effectively plan and carry out the grant or contract requirements.

There are a variety of techniques that can be used to present the project's time-table. Table 9.2 is one of the most common timelines known as a Gantt chart. According to Wikipedia,

> a *Gantt chart* is a type of bar chart, adapted by Karol Adamiecki in 1896 and independently by Henry **Gantt** in the 1910s, that illustrates a project schedule. **Gantt charts** illustrate the start and finish dates of the terminal elements and summary elements of a project. (Gantt Chart, n.d.)

Our chart illustrates 1) the major activities and tasks, 2) the amount of time to be expended on each activity or task, and 3) the activity spread across the contract period. The time period is typically divided into months or quarters, and an activity's begin and end points are depicted with row bars, Xs, or similar markings. Generally, when viewing a timeline, activities are listed in the order in which they will be accomplished (a forward sequence), as shown in Table 9.2.

By examining the project timeline, one sees which activities are to occur within a particular time frame. It is also beneficial to the project director and the staff for

TABLE 9.2 ◆ Project Timeline

Geta Grant Agency

Project Learning for Life Timeline

Fiscal Year July 1, 20xx to June 30, 20xx

Objective	Jul	Aug	Sep	Oct	Nov	Dec	Jan	Feb	Mar	Apr	May	Jun
Obj.1.1: 50% of 200 low-income school-age children will improve their grade level by one full level												
Send out recruitment materials	X	X				X	X	X	X			
Identify and select assessment protocols	X	X										
Assess students and pretest		X	X	X	X	X	X	X	X			
Train tutors		X	X									
Match tutors and students			X	X	X	X	X	X	X			
Conduct tutoring			X	X	X	X	X	X	X	X	X	X
Evaluation				X				X			X	X

TABLE 9.3 ● Condensed Version of Timeline

Geta Grant Agency
Project Learning for Life Timeline
Fiscal Year July 1, 20xx to June 30, 20xx

Activity	Time
Hire Staff	July 1 to July 30
Train Staff and Volunteers	August 1 to September 15
Develop Curriculum and Evaluation	July 1 to September 30
Schedule Workshops	August 14 to September 30
Conduct Workshops	October 1 to May 30
Conduct Evaluation	October 1 to May 30
Prepare Final Report	June 1 to June 25

monitoring the completion of tasks. Some funders require quarterly reports, and from the timeline chart, they are able to determine what you plan to accomplish each quarter. It is a good idea to include the preparation of any reports to the funder as an activity on the chart.

If there are few activities or the project has a relatively short time span, you can use a more condensed version of the timeline (see Table 9.3).

SCOPE OF WORK FORMS

Many state agencies require a Scope of Work form that provides the basis for the legal contract. This format is useful for conceptualizing the parts of the project for it shows the relationships among the goals, the objectives, the activities and staff responsible for the activities, a timeline, and evaluation. Of course, this is somewhat redundant to the narrative, but it does offer the advantage of a quick synopsis of each objective, implementation activity, timeline, and evaluation. The Scope of Work form in Figure 9.1 is a fairly standard form that requires an applicant to fill it out as is to recreate a matching form on your computer.

As you study the Scope of Work form, you will notice that the goal is written across the top of the page and is numbered (e.g., Goal #1). You will notice that there is also a *contract number* and *agency number* across the top right of the form. Those will be filled in by the funder if you get a contract.

FIGURE 9.1 ◆ Sample Scope of Work Form

Contractor: <u>Geta Grant Agency</u>

Contract Number: _____

Agency Number: _____

Scope of Work

County: <u>Grant County</u>

The Contractor shall work toward achieving the following goals and will accomplish the following objectives. This shall be done by performing the specified activities and evaluating the results using the listed methods to focus on process or outcome.

Goal No. 1 (specify): To insure that all children receive a quality education.

Measurable Objectives	Implementation Activities	Timeline	Methods of Evaluating Process or Outcome Objectives
Obj. 1.1: Two hundred (200) low-income schoolaged children will improve their grades by 20% by June 30, 20xx.	1.1 A. The educational needs of the children will be assessed. (Learning Specialist, Project Director)	7/1/xx to 11/30/xx	1.1 A. Student grade point averages will be obtained for the quarter prior to tutoring and the quarter following the end of tutoring.
	1.1 B. Assessment instruments will be reviewed and selected. (Learning Specialist)	7/1/xx to 8/31/xx	
	1.1 C. Students will be matched with tutors who will spend approx. 60 hours with them. (Project Director)	10/1/xx to 4/30/xx	If a 20% increase in grades is accomplished, the objective will be met. (Project Director, Learning Specialist)
	1.1 D. Student grade point records will be obtained for evaluation. (Project Director)	10/1/xx to 6/15/xx	

The first column contains an objective that is numbered in sequence relative to the goal for which it applies. A second objective under Goal 1 would be numbered as 1.2 and so on.

The second column identifies the implementation activities that will accomplish the particular objective. It is also customary to provide the job title of the individual(s) responsible for that activity. The numbering that we used in filling out this section is standard.

The third column, the timeline column, indicates the start and end date for each activity. In most cases, you will include the year for both the start and end dates.

The final column is for the evaluation of the objective. You will state how each objective will be measured to determine if it has been achieved. It is typical to close by repeating the outcome goal, for example, if a 20% increase in grades is accomplished, the objective will be met.

There are times when you will need a second page for the same objective, and you can identify it by stating "Obj 1.1 (continued)" in the *measurable objective* column of the form.

KEY POINTS FOR CHAPTER 9

1. An implementation plan describes preparatory, service, and evaluation activities. In describing project activities make sure to provide sufficient detail for the reviewers.

2. A project narrative provides a thorough description of the proposed project including goals, objective, implementation activities, and evaluation plans.

3. There are several acceptable timeline templates for use in a proposal, and the most common is a Gantt chart.

CHAPTER 9 ACTIVITIES

Chapter 9 Activity 1

Create a Scope of Work form on your computer, and fill it in for Goal 1, Objective 1.

What is the timeline for the proposed activities? What staff and technical resources will be required?

Chapter 9 Activity 2

Create a timeline of your project using a Gantt chart.

What activities can be implemented concurrently, and what activities need to be scheduled concurrently? From the past experience, how much time does each activity require? Is the timeline for each activity realistic?

CREATING THE BUDGET AND BUDGET JUSTIFICATION

CHAPTER TOPICS

The Budget Context
Preparation of a Line-Item Budget
Other Types of Budgets
Other Budgeting Issues

THE BUDGET CONTEXT

There is a back-and-forth, give-and-take dance that occurs between the design and cost of the program. Making the program budget forces the grant writer to think as creatively as possible about how to deliver a meaningful and robust program at a price point that will get funded. It challenges the grant writer to think of cost-efficient ways to deliver services such as using volunteers, obtaining donations from the business community, or charging moderate fees to clients when they can afford to pay them. In the real world, it often takes many attempts to determine how best to structure the program staffing as well as the program "deliverables" to keep costs contained. One usually begins thinking about a budget as soon as the amount of funding is known and a general type of project idea becomes evident. Your thinking will be bounded by what the money can buy. Small grants provide less room for a creative program development process to occur. Whatever the size of your project is, the budget should tell the same story in numbers; for example, you might come home driving a new Cadillac, and your spouse may ask what you paid for it. It would be quite unbelievable to say $100.

The same is true for your project budget. The amount of the request must fit the scope of the project. Budgets can also be used as a way to check the feasibility of a project. If you feel that your budget is stretched too thin, and the budget limit imposed by the sponsor can't cover the costs for all planned activities, you can use this as a signal that project activities should be closely reviewed and realigned with available funding.

As you prepare your proposal, you are thinking of many different activities and services that will require funding to deliver. Even programs that rely heavily on volunteers have hard costs, meaning they need cold, hard cash to pay for something. As the grant writer, it will likely be up to you to pull together all of the project expenses to create a budget for the project. If you are working for an agency, you will need to discuss the proposal with the executive director to see how he or she would like the budget compiled. You will most likely work with the finance director, who will work with you to learn about the project and determine what the *direct costs* of that project will be. Direct costs are those expenditures that the agency has determined are directly related to the performance of the project in some way—salaries for employees of the project, materials used in the project, rent, phones, copiers, office supplies, conferences, travel, and mileage to name a few. (Direct costs in federal projects are subject to the allowable, allocable, and reasonable criteria as defined by the Federal Cost Principles in OMB Circular A-21.) In some agencies, direct costs may also include the time of the finance department to manage the cost center of the new project and the time of Human Resources to hire new personnel, for example.

In most agencies, shared costs, or those that cannot be identified with a specific program, are pooled into a category known as *indirect costs*. Indirect costs generally consist of the many services the administrative branch of the agency provides such as administration, accounting, audits, certifications and review, compliance information technology, library, security, depreciation, utilities, building maintenance, and other costs usually related to the cost of business or facilities and administrative (F&A) costs. The agency determines the *indirect rate* charged as a percent of each budget. For example, if the agency has a 20% indirect rate, you will include that in your budget. Some agencies also allow for the indirect costs to be applied to some expenses but not others. For example, the National Institutes of Health (NIH) does now allow indirect costs to be added to equipment purchases. The finance director will most likely tell you what the agency indirect cost rate is and how to calculate it. Some agencies have *negotiated federal rates*. This means that the agency has obtained federal government approval to charge a certain indirect rate on its contracts above the allowable indirect rate. If you are preparing a grant application that restricts the amount of indirect costs or flatly refuses these costs, you will need to include the appropriate indirect expense as direct expenses in your line-item budget. There are two ways you can do this: 1) take the percent your project represents of the total agency cost and use that percentage to get the amount attributable to your project, or 2) take the actual cost of the item.

Finally, if this proposal and budget are being prepared as part of a class assignment, you might rely on a local newspaper or internet searches to come up with ballpark costs: salaries for employees, office space rent, and other costs such as cell phone or equipment, and set an indirect rate at the industry average for your particular industry. Human service agencies may have indirect rates of 10% to 20%, while educational institutions may have rates of 30% to 50%, and if you are making up a proposal for an assignment, then perhaps take a guess using these parameters.

PREPARATION OF A LINE-ITEM BUDGET

A line-item budget is the most common type of program budget, and it is so named because it provides a budget "line" for each type of expenditure. The upper portion of the budget is for personnel costs, and the lower portion for operating expenditures. (There is a line-item budget worksheet in Appendix C.) Table 10.1 presents your first look at a line-item program budget.

As you study this budget, you may have noticed is that there is a column labeled "FTE" in the Personnel section. This stands for *full-time equivalent* meaning 1 FTE = a full-time employee working a 40-hour work week. You will notice that the executive director is listed as a direct personnel expenditure, which means that he or she will spend 0.1 FTE of their time directly on this project in some way (0.1 FTE = 10% of 40 hours or 4 hours a week on this project). The third column is labeled "Monthly Range FTE" and represents the salary range a full-time employee would be paid. As you look at the column and see that the executive director has $800/month of his or her salary paid under this contract, and it represents 10% time, so the executive director must make $8,000 a month. An agency usually has the monthly range for each position it manages on its "Wage and Salary Schedule." You would expect to hire new employees at the lowest end of the range and increase salary over time per the agency schedule. The final column represents a total for the year. (Note: 40 hrs/week x% time = hours/week and 2,080 hrs/yr x% time = hours/year.) Table 10.2 will assist you in calculating FTE.

TABLE 10.1 ⬢ Line-Item Budget

Geta Grant Agency
Parenting Education Project
July 1, 20xx through June 30, 20xx

Personnel	FTE	Monthly Range (FTE)	Monthly	Yearly
Executive Director	0.1	$8,000-$10,000	$900	$10,800
Project Director	1	5,000-6,500	5,000	60,000
Educator	0.5	4,000-5,500	4,000	24,000
Therapist	0.5	4,000-5,500	4,000	24,000
Admin Assistant	0.5	3,000-4,000	3,000	18,000
Subtotal Personnel				**$136,800**
Benefits @ 28%				38,304
Total Personnel				**$175,104**
Operating Expenses				
Communications			$400	$4,800
Rent (500 s.f.x 1.50 psf)			750	9,000
Office Supplies			300	3,600
Printing			200	2,400
Program Materials			300	3,600
Furniture/Fixtures			200	2,400
Equipment Purchase (computer)			100	1,200
Equipment Rental (copier)			90	1,080
Program Liability Insurance			100	1,200
Conference			350	4,200
Mileage at 0.56 (GSA rate)			120	1,440
Subtotal Operating			**$2,910**	**$34,920**
Subtotal Project Budget				**$210,024**
Indirect at 15% Total Budget				31,504
Grand Total				**$241,528**

TABLE 10.2 ● Calculating FTE			
FTE	**Percent Time**	**Meaning**	**Hours per Year**
1	100%	40 hours per week	2,080
0.8	80%	32 hours per week	1,664
0.5	50%	20 hours per week	1,040
0.25	25%	10 hours per week	520
0.10	10%	4 hours per week	208
0.05	5%	2 hours per week	104

What Does a Unit of Service Cost?

The cost of a unit of service varies based on the type of service being delivered. Generally speaking, the higher the level of professional involvement in the service delivered, the higher the cost. Medical care delivered by an M.D. costs more than that delivered by a nurse's aide, for example. For our purposes here, we are going to obtain a cost per unit of service so that we can apply "reasonableness" criteria to the budget. Just as buying a new Cadillac for $100 is unlikely, and unreasonable, we want to assess if it our budgeted amounts are reasonable. To do this, we calculate what it would cost to deliver a unit of service under our contract.

Here's a simple example: The agency is writing a proposal to provide after-school tutoring to 25 teens for 5 days a week over a 13-week spring semester. You determine the project will cost $50,000 to deliver as planned. To determine cost per unit of service, we would divide $50,000 by 25 teens to arrive at cost of $2,000 per teen. If we divide this by 13 weeks, the program costs $154 per teen per week, or $30.80 per day. As the proposed program gives the teens access to credentialed teachers, learning disability specialist, volunteer tutors, and their own workbooks, the price per day is actually less than could be obtained in the community at large. Meaning, if you went into the community and tried to obtain services for one student—you found a tutor (free), bought a workbook ($75/65 days = $1.15/day), paid a teacher ($50/hour who spent 15 minutes a day with this student, costing $12.50) and a learning disability specialist ($60/hr at 15 minutes = $15, rented a site ($100/day x 65 days = $6,500/12 is $541.66 per student/65 days = $8.33 per day), and add staff time to obtain and supervise these services at $32/hour, 3 hours per day, $96/12 = $8/ day for a total of $45. It is clear you would not be able to procure this for $30.80 per day. This example meets the reasonableness criteria.

TABLE 10.3 ● Common Personnel Expenditures		
Executive Director	Finance Director	Human Resources
Project Director	Project Professional Staff	Project Clerical Staff
Payroll Taxes	Clinical Supervision	Employee Health Benefits
Information Technology	Student Interns	Receptionist

Furthermore, the fact that the service is cost-effective can be added into the program narrative to help sell the program idea to the funder.

Personnel expenditures are generally the largest percentage of costs of a project. Table 10.3 shows the common types of personnel expenditures in program budgets and can be used by you in planning the budget.

What kind of staff do you need to run the project? In almost all cases, there will be some combination of the following staffing configuration:

1. A project director who will have overall administrative responsibility for the project and some direct service responsibilities. This individual has the educational background and experience to manage this type of program. In most cases, funders will look for a full-time person in this role, and the agency will depend upon this person to implement the project and follow the budget as approved. The project director will often be responsible to deliver some of the services while managing the project as a whole.

2. The professional staff whose education and expertise anchor the service delivery component of the program. These are the people who deliver the service. Perhaps they will be licensed therapists, counselors, child care providers, credentialed educators, or health care providers.

3. Volunteers who may also be used to deliver services. Perhaps the volunteers will be professionals, paraprofessionals, students, or general community members. Volunteers provide services under the contract for free. This level of staffing often requires a level of recruitment into the project, a training program to prepare them for the delivery of services (and this training should be included in the program design and costs), and supervision. Although there are some costs involved in using interns or volunteers in a project, it is usually a cost-effective manner to deliver services. Plus there are many additional benefits both to the volunteer or intern as the training helps improve the field as a whole as it builds

the capacity of future professionals and builds relationships in the community.

4. Clerical/administrative assistants/receptionists are persons hired to manage phones, paperwork, scheduling, data entry, and other clerical duties for the project.

5. Finance director and accounting staff to establish a cost center for the project, manage the projects finances, pay bills and track expenditures, and prepare financial reports.

6. Most projects add a percentage of time of the executive director to provide supervision to the project director, interact with the funder to negotiate or implement the contract, and ensure fiscal and programmatic compliance. Some projects also include a percentage of the executive director's time to attend community meetings or conduct other public relations efforts of the project.

7. Almost all projects add a human resources director to recruit open positions of the project, provide staff training, and manage employee interactions and benefits.

Employee benefits are also included under "Personnel Costs." The agency will determine what is included in this benefits line. At a minimum, this amount will include employer contributions for federal and state governments (e.g., FICA and Federal Withholding taxes, State Disability Insurance, Medicare, and Social Security contributions). Other employee benefits provided by the employer may also be included on this line and will often include health and dental insurance and retirement funds. The total amount of payroll taxes and benefits provided to the employee is calculated as a percentage of the total salary amount. The benefit amount will vary widely depending on the organization type—many nonprofit social service agencies have benefits calculated closer to 20%–25%, whereas governmental organizations or institutions of higher education may assess benefits up to 30%–50%.

Now let us look at the second section of the budget that addresses operating expenses. Again, it is important to look carefully at the proposal itself and identify all of the items that will cost money. The operating costs listed in Table 10.4 are typical among project proposals.

You will probably notice that we have included consultants in the operating budget and not the personnel budget. In most cases, consultants will be included under

TABLE 10.4 ⬡ Common Operational Costs		
Rent	Utilities	Printing
Office Supplies	Equipment Rental	Equipment Purchase
Communications	Staff Training	Project Materials
Project Liability Insurance	Advertising	Travel
Consultants	Conferences	Mileage

operating budgets as a nonemployee program expenditure. (We would classify a consultant as a nonemployee because they work independently under a consultant contract, are responsible to carry their own liability insurance and health insurance plans, and pay their own taxes on income they make.) In addition, many state and federal funders have established fixed reimbursement rates for things such as mileage, per diem for travel, and consultants, and you will want to carefully read the application for detailed descriptions of what is acceptable. Perhaps other details in the budget will not be apparent until you reach the negotiation stage. For example, you might have $5,000 in the budget to purchase a computer and printer, and during the negotiation, the funder tells you that they will not pay for the purchase of equipment but will allow you to rent it; you can then make the necessary adjustments. *Read* all of the instructions the funder gives on preparing the budget. Most funders state their restrictions in their application package.

Budget Justifications

In addition to writing the line-item budget, many funders want you to provide a detailed narrative on the budget and drill down to what is included on each line and how the totals per line were reached. In a budget justification, each of the lines is explained. The following is an example of a budget justification for a line-item budget.

Budget Justification for Geta Grant Agency

<u>**Personnel**</u>

Executive Director: The agency executive director will be responsible for the supervision of the project director, a small part of community networking, attending the funder's yearly conference, and providing overall program fiscal and operational compliance representing 4 hours a week of her time (.05 FTE), for a total of $9,600 a year.

Project Director: A project director will work full time (100%) on this project with program implementation and evaluation responsibilities, staff and volunteer supervision, and report-writing duties. The project director, who is also a licensed marriage and family therapist, will also provide 10 hours a week of direct service under this contract. The salary is $57,600 per year.

Educator: An educator will work full time to conduct educational evaluations, create specialized learning plans, and conduct one-on-one and group educational programs for the duration of the project for a total of $38,400 per year.

Therapist: A part-time (50% time) therapist will work with the most troubled youth and their parents in in-depth conducting sessions at the program site and work in coordination with the child's teacher and probation officer for a total of $24,000.

Administrative Assistant: An administrative assistant will be assigned 50% time on this project to prepare project correspondence, receive phone calls from interested parents, schedule programs, and respond to questions or requests for information at a total of $21,600 per year.

The Subtotal Personnel Is $146,400.

Employee benefits have been calculated at 25%, which includes FICA and Federal Withholding, State Disability Insurance, State Withholding, Medicare, Worker's Compensation and Health, Vision, and Dental Benefits. The total benefits for this project is $48,960.

Total Personnel Costs Are $183,000.

Operating Expenses

Communications has been calculated at $500/month to include $180/month for three landline phones in the office; $60 per month for three cell phones for the project director, educator, and therapist so that they are available during and after work hours, usage $70; and internet connection $70 for a total of $6,000 per year.

Rent has been calculated at $1.50 per square foot times 500 square feet of space for a total of $750 per month times 12 months, totaling $9,000. Utilities are included in rent pricing.

Office Supplies are $400 per month and include six-part file folders on each participant, notebooks, locking tote boxes to transport files between sites, paper, pens, copier toner, printer ink, desk supplies, phone supplies, and receipt books for a total of $4,800/year.

Travel Expenses include mileage to and from school sites, homes, and community meeting places for an estimated 100 miles per staff, or 300 miles per month at 0.56 cents per mile times 12 months for a total of $2,016 per year. (See the IRS website for updated Standard Mileage Rates: https://www.irs.gov/tax-professionals/standard-mileage-rates.) Also included in travel is $852 per person for transportation and per diem (at State Board of Control rates) to one major conference for two staff members. The total request for travel is $3,720.

Printing is calculated at $150/month to provide worksheets for the youth classroom exercises, announcements for students and parents, the monthly newsletter, and parenting newsletters throughout the year for a yearly total of $1,800.

Vehicle Expenses: A vehicle (small bus) will be leased for a total of eight trips at $450/trip for a total of $3,600. The vehicle will be used to transport students and faculty on educational field trips. The cost of the vehicle includes insurance and a driver with a Class B license.

Insurance (auto) includes an additional $75 per trip to provide student and faculty health insurance riders and coverage of their belongings for a total of $600 a year.

General Liability coverage for the program for all students, staff, volunteers, and guests on the premises will be $200/month or $2,400 a year.

Client Incentives are used to reward students who are climbing the ladder to success. Students will receive backpacks, iPods, and educational games for a total of $1,800 per year.

Educational Materials include textbooks, curriculum units for the educator, and materials that the therapist needs to work effectively with the children at $400/month for a total of $4,800/year.

Furniture includes desks, bookcases, tables, and chairs at $300/month for a total of $3,600/year.

Equipment Rental applies to the copier lease at $400/month. The lease includes copier maintenance quarterly for a total of $4,800/year.

Equipment Purchase includes the purchase of three iPads to be used by the educator, therapist, and project director for a total of $1,500 and one desktop computer at $300 for the administrative assistant for a total of $1,800.

The Total Operating Costs Are $48,324.

Indirect costs are charged to this project at 15% of the project total $266,023 at $34,699 to provide reimbursement for administrative overhead for the project.

The Total Budget for This Project Is $266,023.

OTHER TYPES OF BUDGETS

Some foundations and nonprofit trusts require a more simplified budget in which you indicate expense categories rather than itemizing line by line. The budget in Table 10.5 combines line-item categories into more general categories. This type of budget provides the agency with much more flexibility in the actual allocation of expenses, and it is usually possible for the agency to transfer funds between lines without contacting the funder.

Matching Funds and In-Kind Budgets

When some of the costs of the project will be assumed by the agency, the agency is said to be contributing this money *in-kind* or as *a cost share*, and this portion of agency-borne expense is indicated in the budget. The funding for an in-kind contribution may come from the agency's fundraising efforts, from other funding sources that are devoted to these services, through the receipt of product and services from the community, and through its use of volunteers, allowing it to reduce costs.

Other funding sources may require that the agency provide *matching funds* of a certain percent of the amount requested. For example, one state office offered to fund 75% of the cost of providing a case management system to pregnant and parenting teens and required the applicant to provide a 25% match. An agency needs to determine what existing funds can be used to provide a match in this

TABLE 10.5 ● Simplified Budget	
Geta Grant Agency Parenting Education Project Budget July 1, 20xx through June 30, 20xx	

Personnel	
Salaries	$136,800
Benefits @ 28%	38,304
Subtotal Personnel	$175,104
Operating Expenses	
Overhead	$31,504
Program	29,280
Travel and Conferences	5,640
Subtotal Operating Expenses	$66,424
Total Budget Request	$241,528

contract, or develop a way to bring in additional funds to meet the match. In both cases, whether *in-kind, cost-share*, or *matching funds*, the funder expects that it will receive full credit for the number of clients to be served under the project and that the clients should not be "double counted" for services elsewhere. In other words, you can't count clients whose service is *fully* funded under one contract to meet the goals of another contract.

The example in Table 10.6 indicates one way to present an in-kind budget. The first column indicates the funder's portion of the total request, the second column indicates the agency's portion, and the third column indicates the total to be allocated for each item. Note: A similar format can be used if you are writing a proposal in which the resources are coming from more than one funder. Indicate the source of the funding in each column, followed by a total funding column.

(As you may also be interested in applying for federal funding, we have included a copy of the budget forms used in federal proposals in Appendix C.)

OTHER BUDGETING ISSUES

Budget Adjustment

At times during the contract year, changes may need to be made in the budget. These changes are usually due to a desire to reallocate savings in one area to

TABLE 10.6 ● Match or "In-Kind" Budget

Geta Grant Agency
Budget Request
July 1, 20xx to June 30, 20xx

Personnel	FTE	Yearly Salary	Funding Request	Match	Total
Executive Director	.05	$60,000	$2,000	$1,000	$3,000
Project Director	1.0	42,000	38,000	4,000	42,000
Clerical	.50	25,044	12,522	0	12,522
Accounting	.10	48,000	0	4,800	4,800
Subtotal Salaries			$52,522	$9,800	$62,322
Benefits @ 20%			10,504	1,960	12,464
Total Personnel			$63,026	$11,760	$74,786
Operating Expenses					
Rent			4,000	5,360	$9,360
Office Supplies			1,500	300	1,800
Printing			2,200	600	2,800
Equipment Rent/Maint.			2,800	400	3,200
Telephone			2,000	400	2,400
Travel			2,000	580	2,580
Subtotal Operating			$14,500	$7,640	$22,140
Total Budget Request			**$77,526**	**$19,400**	**$96,926**

cover overages in another. Some funders will allow for a transfer between line items to a small extent without their approval, but in most cases, the funder will request the grantee to engage in a notification and approval process plan. This process of requesting a transfer of money between the lines is called a *budget adjustment.*

As you will see in Table 10.7, "Budget Adjustment," one column lists the current contract totals for the year, another indicates the amount of money you want to add or subtract from the column, and the final column indicates the new totals. With budget adjustments, you are not changing the total amount that you have to work with but reallocating the money between lines.

TABLE 10.7 ⬡ Budget Adjustment			
	Prior Approved Amount	**Adjustment Effective 10/1/20xx**	**New Approved Amount**
Personnel			
Executive Director	$2,000	(100)	$1,900
Project Director	38,000	0	38,000
Clerical	12,522	0	12,522
Benefits	10,504	(20)	10,484
Total Personnel	$63,026	(120)	$62,906
Operating Expenses			
Rent	$4,000	0	$4,000
Office Supplies	1,500	500	2,000
Printing	2,200	(380)	1,820
Equipment Rental Maintenance	2,800	(500)	2,300
Telephone	2,000	0	2,000
Travel	2,000	500	2,500
Subtotal Operating	14,500	120	14,620
Total Budget	$77,526	0	$77,526

The adjusted budget will most often need to have a written explanation attached, which describes what has happened, on a per line basis, to necessitate the request for a change. In the explanation, you will tell the funder why there is excess money in some lines and the cause of a deficit in others. The funder will be looking for a legitimate rationale to move funds between lines.

Budget Amendment

If, during the course of the contract, your Scope of Work has been expanded or reduced, you may need to do a budget amendment reflecting this change. A simple way to think about this is: When you need to shift money and it does not alter the Scope of Work in any way, you write an adjustment. If something has happened to significantly alter the scope—for example, the funder has asked you to take on an additional project or activity and will provide more money—you will write an amendment. Some funders require an amendment if you are seeking to move more than $5,000 (or some other predetermined amount). Amendments are usually written using the same budget format for requesting adjustments.

The major difference between an amendment and an adjustment is that the amendment changes your contract with the funder and goes through a formal approval process. You will receive a new copy of the contract with the amended budget and any program changes resulting from the amendment.

Contract Negotiations and Subcontracting

It will be a good day when the agency is notified that the proposal has been approved for funding. If the funding is less than requested, you will most likely reconvene with the team to discuss the changes that will need to be made to the budget and program. As the grant writer, you are in a key position to know how the budget affects the program and vice versa. Be conscious of the possible "domino" effect that a change in the budget will have on the entire program and develop a few possible changes to the proposal that will meet the funder's request. Discuss these changes with your team and prepare to 1) attend the contract negotiation session or 2) submit the changes to the funder directly.

If there is a formal contract negotiation, you, and most likely a senior agency administrator, will meet face-to-face with the funder, review what is going to be provided by the contract, review the changes that reduced funding has made to the proposal, and answer other questions the funder may have. The funder may want to ask questions about the project or make changes to the project. Always approach these negotiations carefully because it can be easy to make changes in a project that will be difficult to live with.

No one knows the project better than you. Approach the negotiations from the perspective of win-win. The funder wants a good program just as you do. Here are a few guidelines for negotiating contracts:

1. Reread the proposal prior to going into the negotiations. Be intimately familiar with all of it as you were when writing it 6 months ago.

2. Create an atmosphere of partnership with the contract negotiator.

3. Take your time when you make changes. Look at the impact any change will have on the objectives even if this means that you ask for additional time to consider the impact of the requested changes on the project.

4. Be prepared to discuss your rationale for keeping the project as initially developed in the proposal, and don't be too anxious to change it.

5. If the agency has not been awarded the full amount requested, prepare a new version of the proposal in advance of the meeting. This enables you

to have time to rethink the budget and program and decide upon the revisions that make the most sense to you.

6. Remember to maintain your integrity. If you know that the agency cannot do the job for the amount of money offered, say so. In this case, the agency will need to decide if it is worth pursuing. It is possible, and we have seen it happen, that the agency will choose to turn down the contract because accepting it would be too costly to the agency.

Subcontracting

Subcontracting means that your agency receives the master contract from the funder. This makes your agency the primary contractor or the "lead agency." The lead agency then prepares *subcontracts* for the other agency involved in the project. This is a typical arrangement used by a collaborative or by two or more community agencies in partnership. The subcontracting agency is bound by the same contractual terms as the primary contractor. The primary contractor is responsible for ensuring that the subcontracting agency abides by the terms of the contract and usually prepares a legally binding agreement to this effect. (For a more in-depth treatment of the topic of contracts and subcontracting, see Kettner et al., 2016.)

If you are using subcontractors, you have to address this issue within the body of the grant itself to clearly identify by objectives the role of the subcontractor in the contract and to establish the credibility of the subcontractor in the applicant capability section. The budget of the subcontractor is included in the main budget and fully described in the budget justification.

As you review the steps in budget preparation, you can see why this should not be left to the last minute. Preparing the budget requires that you have a thorough grasp of the project, including all of the details of the implementation activities, so that you can be certain not to omit any major costs. *Remember: Changes in the program will have an impact on the budget, and changes in the budget will have an impact on the program.*

KEY POINTS FOR CHAPTER 10

1. Budget information is included both in table form and as a narrative. The budget narrative is an explanation of how you arrived at each number on the budget. Both table and narrative parts should present the same information about projected expenses.

2. Some sponsors may have limitations on what costs can be included as direct expenses. Make sure to review budget guidelines, and discuss any concerns with the potential funder.

3. Budgets expenditures may change during the term of the contract, and changes may require either a simple budget adjustment or a formal change in the budget through an amendment.

CHAPTER 10 ACTIVITIES

Chapter 10 Activity 1

Consider that you are developing a training project and need to estimate the cost of renting facilities to conduct workshops. Apply this scenario to a topic that is relevant to your interests.

- What possibilities do you have for training space rental? Donation of training space?
- What facilities can be rented free of charge and under what conditions?
- What facilities will require a rental fee?

Chapter 10 Activity 2

Make a spreadsheet in which you create a simple line-item budget for your household operating expenses. Create simple categories: Food, Utilities, Rent/Mortgage, Clothing, Medical, Phone.

Enter your monthly and yearly amounts. (Learn how to enter a formula to calculate for you.)

How are the costs estimated? What past activities can serve as an example?

OTHER PROPOSAL COMPONENTS AND FINISHING TOUCHES

This chapter provides an overview of what some refer to as the *finishing touches* of the proposal. These are the items that complete the proposal and are often prepared after the main sections have been written. You will want to follow the funder's guidelines regarding what items are requested and acceptable to attach to the proposal in an appendix, and often these include the following:

1. Project Abstract

2. Agency Capability Statement

3. Letters of Support

4. Developing the Memorandum of Understanding (MOU)

5. Documents to Be Attached: List of board members, audited financial statements, current budget, organizational chart, the agency IRS 501(c)(3) letter, and so on

As you near the home stretch of proposal preparation, there are some important "last" pieces that become part of the proposal document. We address those components with examples in the following discussion.

PROJECT ABSTRACT

Most funders will ask for a 100-word abstract (or some other word-limited statement) of the proposed project. You may be surprised by all of the things this little abstract will be asked to do:

- Serve as an overview of the project to the funder during review

- Be highlighted on the funder's website of funded projects

- Be incorporated into the contract and used to track overall progress

- Be used to develop publicity for the project

It is important to give this abstract a lot of thought. It should capture the details of the project such as the following:

- What is the goal of the project

- Who is being served (including eligibility) and in what number

- What services will be delivered

- Where will the services be delivered

- How will success be measured

- What is the budget

Sample Project Abstract

The Share Ourselves Agency has successfully served 4,100+ youth and parents in the Auburn community over the past 10 years. Project Better Outcomes addresses an urgent need to improve oral health among school-age children, 90% of whom have never seen a dentist. Project one provides six dental clinics for low-income youth (one at each elementary school) in the Auburn area. Eight hundred students will receive tooth cleaning, screening, and hygiene kits; 400 students will receive fillings. Project two targets 40 high-risk adolescents to receive educational assessments and provides each student with 40 hours of need-specific tutoring after school to raise their school performance by one full grade level. Both projects will utilize parent and college-age volunteers working with professional staff to deliver services. The budget request is $285,000.

AGENCY CAPABILITY STATEMENT

Almost all proposals require an agency capability statement (or applicant capability statement). In this statement, the agency presents its history and qualifications to the funder. Now that you understand the history and mission of the agency, as well as some of its program offerings of the present and past, it is a good time to start writing the agency capability statement. Of course, you will need to fine-tune this statement once the entire proposal is completed to ensure that you have highlighted the appropriate agency experience and described the current proposal accurately.

The agency capability statement establishes an organization's credibility to successfully undertake the project. It indicates who is applying for the grant, what qualifies an agency to conduct the project, and what resources (e.g., organizational, community) are available to support the effort. This section helps generate confidence that the agency is programmatically competent and qualified to address the need/problem and that the agency is fiscally sound and able to manage the contract responsibly.

In developing this section, the grant writer will want to capture the way that the agency sees itself as well as the way its clients and the community view it. Consider and collect the following information to help in writing the agency capability statement:

- Agency brochures and pamphlets as well as annual reports

- Applicant capability statements from other grant applications

- Client testimonials

- Previous evaluation measures that indicate client satisfaction

A good capability statement should accomplish two things: 1) it should describe the agency's characteristics and its track record, and 2) it should demonstrate how those qualities make them qualified to undertake the proposed project. Many times, grant writers accomplish the first task but leave it up to the reviewers to infer the latter. They often fail to present a cogent argument that connects what they have done with what they are now proposing to do.

When writing this section, avoid overusing the words *we* and *our*. It is appropriate to refer to the name of the agency or simply write *the agency* throughout the text. Write as if you are developing a public relations article for a national newsletter, informing the reader, making it interesting but brief. The writing style should be clear and concise, and avoid acronyms, abbreviations, and jargon as much as possible.

If the agency is serving as a lead agency for a collaborative effort, you would highlight the agency's experience and also include subsections on each of the other agencies involved. It is customary to ask the participating agency to write their own capability sections to include in the proposal. A typical agency capability statement will reflect much of the following information:

1. *Mission of the Agency*—the overall philosophy and aims of the organization and vision for the agency

2. *History of the Agency*—a brief overview of when, why, and how the agency started and whether its focus has changed over time

3. *Organizational Resources*—a description of the agency's funding track record and of the human and material resources available to this project (Include the pertinent background of staff, especially expertise in areas related to the need/problem, other professionals associated with the agency, and any special equipment, materials, and services which can support the proposed project)

4. *Community Recognition and Support*—an indication of how the agency is regarded, including awards, accreditations, and honors bestowed upon it and the staff, as well as how the community is involved in the agency's operation and structure (e.g., through membership, in programs, on committees, and boards)

5. *Interagency Collaboration and Linkages*—a depiction of the linkages and support available from other organizations that can assist with the proposed project, including memberships in local, state, and national networks

6. *Agency Programs*—an overview of the unique programmatic contributions the agency makes to its clients and the community, including the aims and types of programs, and a quantitative picture of what is accomplished (e.g., the numbers served, the distribution rate of materials, the cost savings resulting from these services, and program outcomes)

7. *Agency Strengths*—a description of the organizational characteristics
   that make the agency particularly suited to implement the project. In
   general, you indicate what is being proposed and how that fits with what
   the organization already has accomplished. For example, the agency may
   already be serving the target group, or addressing the need/problem, or
   using a particular technique or strategy that it now wishes to modify
   or implement in a different manner. Provide the agency web address
   somewhere in the agency capability statement.)

Sample Agency Capability Statement

The nationally recognized and regionally acclaimed Boys and Girls Clubs of
Nirvana has provided 38 years of service to youth in the greater Nirvana area. The
mission of the agency is to "improve the physical well-being and quality of life for
boys and girls living in Nirvana." The agency's staff of 15 youth workers, seven
area managers, and executive director have offered programs to more than 1,200
youth per year. In addition, the agency has more than 40 volunteer tutors who
provide at least 5 hours a week each of service to the youth.

Boys and Girls Clubs of Nirvana partner with several other community youth-serving organizations: the LookOut, Okay to Learn School, and Happy Kickers link
with the agency to expand and enhance program offerings. Current programs
offered by the agency include after-school tutoring, physical education programs,
and nutrition programs to help youth overcome the impact of poverty on their
lives. Program outcomes indicate that 89% of the youth in the agency's programs
have improved their grades by at least one full grade level, and 92% have improved
their overall fitness ranking by one full level after participating in the program.
These outstanding results help guarantee the youth will progress satisfactorily
through school and be prepared for a healthy future. (More program information
can be found on our website at www.boysandgirlsclub.org.)

The proposed program targets extremely high-risk youth and mobilizes services
for them and their parents. The project will provide 100 families with increased
nutritional support through donations from XXX Grocery Store distributed by
the agency, tutoring services 5 days a week, and a family ombudsman who makes
weekly visits to assist the family to obtain needed services.

The Boys and Girls Club of Nirvana is prepared to conscientiously address the
multiple problems faced by needy families in Nirvana and has received the presti-
gious County of Nirvana Supervisor's Award, the State of Nirvana's Youth Angel
Award, and the National Best Boy's and Girl's Club Award. Program staff have the

expertise and experience to build the required relationships with youth and their families. One of the parents served has said, "Boys and Girls Club of Nirvana has helped my children learn. They get better grades at school now. They help me feel more comfortable to talk to the teachers. I am happy they are here!"

SUSTAINABILITY STATEMENT

Sponsors may require a proposal to include a sustainability statement to ensure that the organization has a plan to continue the project beyond the funding period. The statement should describe the accountability and commitment to the project and also the support and infrastructure that is available to carry out continuous activities. Resources to support the sustainability of a project may come from planned fundraising, future grant writing, or sales and services. Depending on the context, a description of the partnership with the community and the transfer of the project ownership to the other local organizations may be appropriate.

Sample Sustainability Statement

We have a long-standing commitment to the planning process as reflected in our strategic plan. Our specific sustainability plan for this project includes two objectives. First, we will engage project stakeholders to secure funding for the XXX activity. We will contact community champions and organize a workgroup to engage in regular fundraising activities. Second, we will designate 0.5 FTE of the project coordinator's time to work with the community leaders to identify resources and assets that can be pooled together to support ongoing service delivery once the initial service infrastructure is created with the funding from this project. There will be other agency partners interested in buying into this service delivery plan.

LETTERS OF SUPPORT

Letters of support are usually obtained from other agencies, possible clients, and influential community members, including elected officials. It is most usual to make contact with the potential letter writer by phone, explain the project, and ascertain their willingness to write a letter of support. If the response is positive, fax or e-mail a sample letter to them that contains enough details about the project that they can write their letter from it, or simply copy your letter onto their letterhead and sign it. You will also provide the writer with directions as to when the letter is due and how you want to receive the letter—are you going to pick it up, have it mailed to you, or have it faxed to you? Below is a sample of a request for a letter of support:

Sample Letter of Support

Dear Agency Executive Director:

The Geta Grant agency is applying for $100,000 in funding to the Office of Health and Human Services to fund a case management system for the Families First Collaborative. This project, called Management for Health, provides a full-time caseworker to address the mental health, educational, parenting, employment, housing, food, and health needs of the highest-risk Latino and white families in the cities of Lemon, Tangerine, and Banana. We expect that more than 200 families with multiple needs will be served in the first year. In addition, our project will evaluate the effectiveness of case management on health and mental health outcomes with this population.

Agencies included in this collaborative proposal include the Department of Education, A Fine Health Center, the Mental Health Center, the Human Interaction Commission, Housing First, and the Food Bank Distribution Center.

If you see the need for these services in our community, or if you are willing to partner with us in this proposal to provide X, Y, and Z, please write a letter of support addressed to: Joe Smith, Program Officer, Office of Health and Human Services, Department 007, 200 State Lane, Room 123, Our Town, CA 90009. *But, if you are mailing the support letter, please send it to me* at: Mary Grant Writer, Geta Grant Agency, 1111 One Street, This Town, CA 90002. We thank you for your support.

Please call us to pick up the letter by Friday, June 2, 20xx.

Sincerely,
Mary Grant Writer, Project Director

As the grant writer, be prepared to make follow-up phone calls to the agencies to encourage their completion of the letter, answer any questions they may have, and schedule a time to pick up the letter if you are nearing the proposal deadline. It is wise to request the letters early, as you are preparing the other sections of the proposal, to avoid any delay as the proposal deadline approaches. In some instances, you may be asked by the organizations to draft a letter of support for them. This is often ideal because you can be specific about the items you want emphasized by each supporting source.

MEMORANDUM OF UNDERSTANDING (MOU)

The role of any subcontractor under the lead agency should be spelled out in a written agreement. The *Memorandum of Understanding* (MOU—with each letter pronounced separately) is a formal, quasi-legal document that itemizes what each of the parties will do and their relationship to each other and the funder.

Sample MOU

Memorandum of Understanding

This Memorandum of Understanding is entered into on _____ by the Geta Grant Agency, hereafter, the lead agency, and the Boys and Girls Club of Grant City, hereafter, the subcontractor. Funding for this project is provided by the U.S. Department of Health Services under what is to be called the *master contract*, and all parties are responsible to ensure that terms and services are delivered and met as required in the master contract. Funding is contingent upon the continuation of funding through the U.S. Department of Health Services and conditional upon continuation of said funding.

The term of this MOU is from ____ to ____. The subcontractor can submit a bill (in a format determined by the lead agency) on a monthly basis by the sixth of the month for services in the previous month. The subcontractor will be reimbursed in the amount of $100 per client served and will submit documentation of service delivered with each invoice as itemized in Exhibit A attached. In addition, the subcontractor will conduct program evaluation, both formal and informal, as itemized in Exhibit B attached.

A failure to perform under this contract will result in the immediate termination of this agreement and may result in forfeiture of funds received. The parties agree to have disagreements heard by a professional arbiter.

This agreement may be terminated by either party with a 3-month written notice in the case of all other reasons. Notices to either party are to be mailed via U.S. mail to:

Amber Smith, Executive Director

Geta Grant Agency

1111 Grant Way
Grant City, MA 22333

Ray Mellor, Executive Director

Boys and Girls Club of Grant City

4444 Fun Street
Grant City, MA 22333

Signature of one Executive Director _____

Signature of second Executive Director _____

Date:_____

Date:_____

FINISHING TOUCHES

Documents to Be Attached

If possible, create a cover page for each document you attach such as financial statements, board of directors, organizational chart, IRS designation, and so on. This will make it easier for you to ensure that you have attached everything the funder is requesting. Use the application checklist, if one is provided, to ensure all attachments are in place.

Send it off with a flourish, take a nice long breath, and celebrate! It is complete; it is *off* to the *funder*! (Make sure you send the proposal with delivery receipt required if mailed through the U.S. Postal Service, or obtain a tracking receipt from overnight delivery services. If possible, when the grantor's address is nearby, hand deliver the proposal to the funder and obtain a receipt.

And now the wait begins. Remember, 50% of the proposals funded are resubmissions that were denied the first time. This statement is not made to discourage you but, rather, to ground you a bit in the reality of the process. Up to 90% of proposals submitted to the federal government get denied at the first submission. Because this is a highly competitive business, grant writers learn not to take rejection personally. In fact, too much personal investment in the proposal can work to your disadvantage because you may lose the objectivity needed to negotiate the proposal, make modifications, or even learn from mistakes.

If you do receive a rejection notice, take a couple of days before you approach the funder. Once you are rebalanced (and have the frustration out of your voice), see if you can obtain a copy of the scoring of your proposal to see how it ranked in relation to others and to learn what may need to be improved or changed in another submission. Remember, we all have had proposals turned down. The proposals that lose are not necessarily bad ideas or bad proposals. They may not have met the funder's idea for a project, they may have not demonstrated the need that other areas can demonstrate, or they may be ahead of their time. When this happens to you, take a breath, shake it off, and climb back into the writer's seat!

Notification of Funding

What if the proposal is not funded?

This is a difficult pill to swallow, and it can have a negative impact on the grant writer who may be wondering if it was something he or she did or didn't do. Or was it something that was left out? In our experience, the most important thing the grant writer can do now is take a breath, take a walk, and shake it off. If it is possible to learn why the project was not funded, do so, but not right away. Let a couple of days go by so that the "ouch" is lessened. Keep the proposal. You may be updating it for a future submission, using it for future program ideas, or referencing sections for other uses, such as data in the needs section for annual reports or other projects. Most importantly, remember, competition is stiff, and you are not going to be successful with every application.

What if the proposal is funded?

Obviously, it is time to celebrate the promise of funding for a project. The agency executive director is usually the designated contact, and he or she will be contacted first. If, by chance, the grant writer learns first, contact the agency executive director and the project director before saying anything.

The grant writer may be asked to make the phone calls to the partner agencies to let them know the project is funded. You may also want to prepare a press release and give it to the project director to submit to local newspapers so the community will know about the funding. This press release and a brief letter should also go to local legislators and the city council so that they can learn of the good your agency is doing through the new funding.

Prepare a thorough, but short, summary of the project to be given to board members or others in the community, especially any agencies or organizations who will benefit from this funding. You also want to prepare a Project Tracking Timeline (see below) indicating the project reporting and evaluation timelines, and if the grant writer is a regular employee of the nonprofit, it helps to create a tickler file of the reporting dates for grants, renewal dates, or other important deadlines.

The computer's calendar can be used for this function by inputting dates into the future that need to be remembered. It will be helpful to send out reminders to the project director of upcoming due dates.

Sample Project Tracking Form

Project Reporting Timeline for: Healthy Families

Project Director: Mary Smith

Funder: **Contact Name:**   **Phone:**

Address: **Email:**   **Fax:**

Funding Period: January through December 20xx

Reports Due on: April 10, July 10, October 10, and Final Report due January 10, 20xx

Evaluation:

- Pre- and posttests for all participants to demonstrate knowledge gain

- Documentation of client participation using sign-in sheets

- Completion of GPRA forms on 50% of all clients

- Follow-up phone calls to determine client satisfaction on 20% of all clients

Billing:

Submitted monthly in arrears of service delivery using funder-developed forms.

Resilience and Dealing With Rejection

Grant funding is competitive, and as a result, you are likely to experience many unfunded applications and the subsequent feelings of rejection that all grant writers feel. It may help to keep in mind that many times the rejection is not an indication that your project is not worthy of investment but rather a shortage of funds. Still, receiving a rejection is hard. To deal with it, consider three strategies that have helped us: 1) go for a walk before talking to anyone about it so you have time to come to grips with your own feelings in private and not in front of a team in a meeting, and 2) be willing to follow up to see who got funded and why. Most funders are willing to share their process with you and will tell you where your proposal was not as competitive as others. This will help you grow in skill and build those valuable relationships at the same time. The third strategy is to have a group of friends who can commiserate with you, with hopefully at least one other grant writer in the group. Keep a list of all of the grants you write and outcome of the submission, along with the funding amounts the agency received. Your portfolio of successful grant applications will rise into the millions of dollars by the end of your career.

KEY POINTS FOR CHAPTER 11

1. An Agency Capability statement describes the applicant's history and qualifications. Write this statement as though you are writing a press release about the organization, and make it interesting.

2. A funder's requirements for proposal contents may vary. The most common proposal components are need statement, project description, budget and description, and evaluation. Be sure to read the RFA carefully.

CHAPTER 11 ACTIVITIES

Chapter 11 Activity 1

Write a 100-word or a 250-word abstract of your proposal. Share it with someone and ask for feedback using the questions below.

Is the goal of the project clear? Are the services and the target community well defined? Are the outcomes impactful?

Chapter 11 Activity 2

Identify a prospective collaborator and write a request for a letter of support.

What are the relevant qualifications and background of the collaborator?

What are the key aspects of the project for which you seek support?

ESTIMATING TIME

In this section, we have provided for the beginning grant writer an illustration of the process involved in calculating a staff person's time expenditure on a project. Let's suppose that Geta Clinic wants to provide an AIDS-prevention education program in the county schools. The objective states:

> Three thousand (3,000) at-risk youth will increase their knowledge by 30% on HIV transmission and risk-reduction behaviors by June 30, 20xx.

The implementation activities with staff responsibilities include the following:

1. Relationship established with schools (Project Director, Community Educator)

2. Education programs developed and scheduled (Community Educator, Administrative Assistant)

3. Parent orientation nights planned and conducted (Community Educator)

4. Two 1-hour educational presentations provided in the students' regular classrooms on the nature of HIV transmission, risky behaviors, decision-making skills, and assertiveness training (Community Educator)

5. Student evaluation using pre- and posttest to indicate knowledge change (Community Educator, Administrative Assistant)

Someone without any knowledge about community education might say:

> Okay, this is simple. An average class size would be 25. Divide 3,000 youths by 25 per class to find out how many actual classes you need; that equals 120 classes. Because the educator will spend 2 hours in each class, that is a total of 240 teaching hours. If I divide 240 hours by 8 hours/day, then I need a community educator for 30 days.

This reasoning process is *faulty* for a number of reasons. What factors need to be considered when implementing a community education program for Geta Clinic? The following discussion will provide an example of the kind of thinking-through process needed to develop a more realistic estimate of the time it will take.

ACCESS TO THE COMMUNITY

Has the clinic ever provided educational programs in the schools? How much time will it take to develop the necessary relationships with the schools to gain access? How much time will be spent scheduling programs? How much time in community relations to develop the network? Will the sensitive nature of the topic affect this development time by making it even more difficult to gain access to the classroom?

SERVICE PREPARATION, EVALUATION, AND DOCUMENTATION

How much preparation will be required to provide the educational program in addition to the direct teaching time? Will the educator need to write the curriculum? Will he or she also need to evaluate the program's effectiveness? Grade the evaluation exams? Maintain other program records? Develop handouts for classroom use?

GEOGRAPHIC LOCATION

How many sites can be reached in a day? Consider the traffic patterns, distance, and climate, for example.

ETHNIC, CULTURAL, AND LINGUISTIC CONSIDERATIONS

Will the clinic need educators from different ethnic backgrounds? What languages will need to be spoken? Written? Is a special knowledge required to work with this specific population(s), and, if so, how much time will it take for the educator to acquire that?

HUMAN CAPABILITY

Finally, consider what is humanly possible to require of a community educator in terms of actual teaching within a given day or week. The energy required in the classroom when the speaker is an outsider is considerably greater than when the audience is familiar with the person. Once the program has gained access to the schools, perhaps one 2-hour presentation per day is all you can reasonably expect someone to do and maintain enthusiasm in the process.

PUTTING IT ALL TOGETHER

Now it is time to recalculate the amount of time required from the educational staff. A full-time employee works 2,080 hours per year. You have determined that the educator will need to spend time developing relationships with the schools. You might estimate that it will take approximately 8 hours of contact time on the phone and in person per school that you want to reach. There are 50 high schools, and therefore, to contact each high school, it would entail about *400 hours.*

Then you calculate that it will take the educator approximately 2 to 3 weeks full time to review the materials that are available and plan the curriculum. If portions of the curriculum need to be written or evaluation tools developed, it would take, you estimate, about 1 month or *174 hours.*

We already know that the teacher will spend 240 hours in the classroom. He or she will go to 120 different classes, and let's say you estimate that it will take 30 minutes travel time each way, so that is another 120 hours in traveling time. So the time spent in classroom presentations and travel time totals *360 hours.*

You have also calculated that it will take the educator approximately 1 hour per class to handle the evaluation component, which equates to another *120 hours.* You also want the educator to have a minimum of 10 hours per month to improve his or her skills and knowledge, update records, attend an in-service training or other meetings, and respond to correspondence, which adds up to another *120 hours* for a total of *240 hours* associated with conducting the evaluation.

Finally, let's add the fact that, due to the sensitive nature of the materials to be addressed in the classroom, the community educator will also need to be involved in making a presentation at parent's night so that they may review materials and ask questions. This will require 2 hours at 50 schools for another *100 hours* plus the 1 hour travel time for *50 hours.* There will be networking with other community groups and involvement on task forces or committees, which take another 5 hours per month or *60 hours* per year. That's a total of *210 hours.*

The total number of hours involved in the community educator's work comes to *1,384 hours for the project year.* There are 2,080 hours in a work year.

Some planners will tell you that once you have made your best time estimate, it is wise to add an *additional 25%* or, in this case, an additional *520 hours*. The reasoning behind this is that things will always take more time than you think, and there will inevitably be delays. In the case of the Geta Clinic, it appears that it would be wise to hire a full-time educator (100%) to reach 3,000 teens with an AIDS prevention program.

In the way that we have conceptualized the job now, the educator will spend the first 4 to 5 months preparing to teach and making contacts with the schools, and the remaining 7 months of the project year providing the actual service. The factors we have included in calculating the amount of time an educator would spend to reach 3,000 teens should follow the implementation activities fairly closely. These calculations will also be needed as you determine the cost of the project. Often, as the true extent of time and effort needed are revealed, the implementation activities or the objectives may need to be modified.

FUNDING RESOURCE INFORMATION

What follows are common sources of information on funding resources that you might find helpful. This is a selective listing; for a more complete picture of funding opportunities, you can consult your local library, or contact one of the following organizations/websites:

Grants.gov

This website provides a website for federal agencies to post funding opportunities and to assist grantees to find and apply for them.

Web address: http:/www.grants.gov

Grants, Etc.

The University of Michigan's website offers access to funding sources, in-kind resources, electronic journals, how-to guides, and other valuable resources.

Web address: http://www.ssw.umich.edu/resources/index2.html?collection=grants

The Grantsmanship Center

This organization has an extensive inventory of funding information, publishes a newspaper for grant-seeking organizations, conducts national training on proposal writing and other areas of human service administration, conducts workshops on grant writing, offers consulting services, and offers a grant database.

Mailing Address: P.O. Box 17220; Los Angeles, CA 90017

Physical Address: 350 South Bixel St., Suite 110; Los Angeles, CA 90017

Web Address: http://www.tgci.com

The Foundation Center

This independent, national service organization was established by foundations to provide an authoritative source of information on private philanthropic giving; publishes directories and guides on foundations; and has established a national network of reference collections through local and university libraries, community foundations, and nonprofit organizations.

Mailing Address: 79 Fifth Avenue/ 16th Street; New York, NY 10003

Web Address: http://www.fdncenter.org

Internet Addresses of Selected Federal and State Funders

Catalog of Federal Domestic Assistance: www.cfda.gov

Grants.gov: www.grants.gov

Housing and Urban Development Grants: www.hud.gov/grants

National Institute for Health (NIH): www.nih.gov

Substance Abuse and Mental Health Services Administration: www.samhsa.gov

United States Department of Health and Human Services: www.dhhs.gov

United States Department of Education: www.ed.gov

Major Publications

Annual Register of Grant Support. Information Today, Inc., 143 Old Marlton Pike, Medford, NJ 08055

Catalog of Federal Domestic Assistance. Superintendent of Documents, U.S. Government Printing Office, 732 North Capitol Street, NW, Washington, DC 20402

Federal Grants and Contracts Weekly. John Wiley and Sons, Inc., 111 River Street Hoboken, NJ 07030

Federal Register. Superintendent of Documents, U.S. Government Printing Office, 732 North Capitol Street, NW, Washington, DC 20402

Publications of the Foundation Center, 79 Fifth Avenue/16th Street, New York, NY 10003

Foundation Directory

Foundation Directory Supplements

Foundation Grants to Individuals

National Directory of Corporate Giving

The Foundation Center's Guide to Proposal Writing

The Grantseeker's Guide to Winning Proposal's

Foundation Fundamentals

Computerized Searches and Databases

There are a number of computerized search services available that provide funding resource information. The advantage of such databases is that they can subdivide and index the funding information into a range of subjects and categories (e.g., by subject, by geographic area). The costs can vary, and some of the information overlaps in the different databases. Check your local university library for more information about services. (Library tip: If you are no longer a student and want to use a university library, check to see if they have a Friends of the Library program. You may be able to join for a reasonable amount per year through this fundraising arm of the library.)

Dialog's Information Retrieval Service is among the largest databases covering a broad range of topics. Among the funding-related databases in the service are the following:

- Federal Register Abstracts

- Federal Research in Progress

- Foundation Directory

- Foundation Grants Index

Computerized searches are also useful for readily identifying literature and data for the needs/problem statement section of the proposal. You might find journal articles or other educational resources at such sites as these:

- PsycINFO database

- ERIC

- EbscoHOST database: Social Science Abstracts

- Medline/PubMed

- Nexis Lexis

Online Journals and Newsletters

- *Chronicle of Philanthropy*: http://www.philanthropy.com

- *Foundation News and Commentary*: http://www.foundationnews.org/

- *Grantsmanship Center Magazine*: http://www.tgci.com/magazine.shtml

General Writing Resources

- Gilman, A. (1995). *Get to the point: How to say what you mean and get what you want.* Kendall Hunt.

- Clark, R. P. (2013). *Help! for writers: 210 solutions to the problems every writer faces.* New York: Little, Brown.

- Casagrande, J. (2010). *It was the best of sentences, it was the worst of sentences.* Ten Speed Press.

APPENDIX C

BUDGET

BUDGET EXERCISE: PREPARING THE PERSONNEL SECTION OF THE BUDGET: FTE AND SALARY RANGE

Full-time Equivalent (FTE)

FTE = Full-time Equivalent: We consider an individual to be a full-time employee if they work 40 hours a week. Forty hours a week is considered to be 100% time, or full-time employment. The number of working hours in a year for a full-time employee is generally calculated at 2,080. A full-time employee represents 1 FTE.

A part-time employee's time is calculated as a percentage of full time; thus, someone working 20 hours a week (1,040 hours per year) is said to be half time, or 0.5 FTE.

Here is how to calculate each of the following:

- FTE: Divide the number of hours worked in a week by 40 hours
- Percentage Time: Move the decimal point two places to the right, hence 0.25 FTE becomes 25%
- Hours Worked per Year: Multiply the FTE x Total Hours in the Year = Hours Worked per Year

How to determine FTE, Percentage Time, Hours per Year—an Example:

Ash works 6 hours a week. Divide 6 by 40 hours = 0.15 FTE

Move the decimal point by two to the right to get percentage time of 15%

Take 0.15 of 2,080 to get Hours per Year (0.15 x 2080) = 312 Hours Worked per Year

You may find the following table useful in calculating FTE and the number of hours that represent work in a year:

FTE	Percent Time	Meaning	Hours per Year
1	100%	40 hours per week	2,080
0.8	80%	30 hours per week	1,664
0.5	50%	20 hours per week	1,040
0.25	25%	10 hours per week	520
0.10	10%	4 hours per week	208
0.05	5%	2 hours per week	104

*This is a fairly standard yearly number of hours worked that includes time off for holidays and vacation days. This can vary based type of employment or country of employment.

Try it Out: List three employees you plan to have in your project.

Job Title	Hrs/Wk	FTE	% Time	Hrs/Yr

Salary Range

Many funders will ask for a salary range in the Personnel section of the budget. The funder wants to see both the bottom and top end of the salary each person can earn.

Employers have a Wage and Salary Schedule for their employees. This is what to use to prepare that section of the budget. A Wage and Salary Schedule ensures that employees are paid equally for time worked in a specific job. The schedule might look roughly something like this:

Job Title	Step One	Step Two	Step Three	Step Four
Project Director	4,000–4,200	4,201–4,411	4,412–4,633	4,634–4,877
Child Care Worker	3,000–3,150	3,151–3,339	3,340–3,567	3,567–3,745
Clerical	2,800–2,940	2,941–3,087	3,088–3,242	3,243–3,405

When a new employee is hired, they usually start at Step One of the Wage and Salary Scale. The starting salary may be adjusted with the step to reflect experience so perhaps the person will start at mid-range of Step One.

Now, let's return to the budget template that you are being asked to fill in and work through it step-by-step:

Personnel	FTE	Monthly Range	Monthly	Yearly

1. Enter job title for personnel and the FTE that they will work on this project.

2. Fill in the "Monthly Range" taken off the Wage and Salary Schedule at the level that this employee is at. For example, if they are new hires, they will start at Step One of the Wage and Salary Schedule, or, if existing employees, use their current step. Put the total full-time Monthly Range here.

3. Monthly: You give the monthly salary amount that will *actually be paid* to this employee. (In real life, you would take an average of the yearly expected salary, taking any raises into consideration, so you will have the correct amount of money to pay this person for the year.)

4. Yearly: Multiply monthly times 12 months.

*If you do not have an idea how much a certain category of employee makes a year, you can conduct a search on the internet by asking "How much does a (insert job type) make a year?"

You will find many salary guides to choose from such as ZipRecruiter, Salary.com, Glassdoor, indeed.com, careerxplorer.com to name a few.

What do you do if you have more than one person working in a certain job classification?

You basically have two options. Under Option 1, if everything is equal among persons in this job category, you could simply increase the FTE to match the total number of employees in this section as well at the total monthly and yearly amounts. Example: You want to hire three clerical staff, each at the same FTE, let's say half time and at the same salary, it would look like this:

Personnel	FTE	Monthly Range	Monthly	Yearly
Clerical	1.5	2,800–2,940	4,200	50,400

Under Option 2, when there are differences in FTE and salary, you would give each a distinct name such as "Clerical A" and "Clerical B" and using a separate line in the budget for each.

Personnel	FTE	Monthly Range	Monthly	Yearly
Clerical A	1	2,800–2,940	4,200	50,400
Clerical B	0.5	2,941–3,087	1,500	18,000

IDENTIFY OPERATING EXPENSES WORKSHEET

Let your mind explore the possible expenses that may be part of the proposed project.

Likely expenses include rent, utilities, janitorial, office supplies, copier, equipment, materials, printing, vehicle, travel, conferences, computer equipment, cameras, phones, furniture, specialty services under contracts such as audits, and insurance.

Here is space for you to write your likely expenses and a column to keep track of these estimated costs. The first line is an example:

Possible Expense	For	Estimated Monthly
Rent	Administrative offices, childcare center, yard	$5,000

Possible Expense	For	Estimated Monthly

BUDGET: A FIRST TRY AT A BUDGET, AKA, "WILL THIS PROJECT WORK?"

Start by sketching out the main expenses for the proposed project:

What	Amount
Subtotal	$

What is the total number of units of direct service under this project _____

Divide the subtotal of the budget by the units of service: _____

*Direct service is face time with the clients/participants in your project. For example, perhaps there are 100 clients who will receive 5 hours each of education for a total of 500 hours of direct services. If the total budget is $200,000, it cost $400 per unit to deliver this service or $2,000 per client.

Now, you must consider if it is worth $2,000 per client, or will you need to modify the project to 1) reach more clients or 2) reduce the costs.

LINE-ITEM BUDGET WORKSHEET

Personnel	FTE	Monthly Range (per 1 FTE)	Monthly Amt (for this position)	Yearly (for this position)
Executive Director				
Project Director				
Educator				
Therapist				
Admin Assistant				
Subtotal Personnel				
Benefits @ ___%				
Total Personnel				
Operating Expenses				
Phones				
Rent (___s. f. x _____per s. f.)				
Internet and Web Hosting				

Office Supplies				
Printing				
Program Materials				
Furniture/ Fixtures				
Equipment Purchase				
Equipment Rental				
Maintenance				
Program Liability Insurance				
Contractors				
Conferences/ Training				
Mileage at _____ per mile				
Subtotal Operating				
Indirect at ___% Total Budget				
Grand Total				

FEDERAL PROPOSAL BUDGET WORKSHEET

We are providing this copy of the federal budget worksheets so that you might see what they look like. You will want to fill these out online while using Grants.gov or another federal portal, and you can find a copy of the SFA 424A at the Office of Management and Budget, Washington DC.

FIGURE AC.1

BUDGET INFORMATION – NON-CONSTRUCTION PROGRAMS

OMB Number: 4040-0006
Expiration Date: 02/28/2022

SECTION A - BUDGET SUMMARY

Grant Program Function or Activity (a)	Catalog of Federal Domestic Assistance Number (b)	Estimated Unobligated Funds		New or Revised Budget		
		Federal (c)	Non-Federal (d)	Federal (e)	Non-Federal (f)	Total (g)
1.		$	$	$	$	$
2.						
3.						
4.						
5. Total		$	$	$	$	$

SECTION B - BUDGET CATEGORIES

6. Object Class Categories	GRANT PROGRAM, FUNCTION OR ACTIVITY				Total [5]
	(1)	(2)	(3)	(4)	
a. Personnel	$	$	$	$	$
b. Fringe Benefits					
c. Travel					
d. Equipment					
e. Supplies					
f. Contractual					
g. Construction					
h. Other					
i. Total Direct Charges (sum of 6a-6h)	$	$	$	$	$
j. Indirect Charges					$
k. TOTAL (sum of 6i and 6j)	$	$	$	$	$
7. Program Income	$	$	$	$	$

SECTION C - NON-FEDERAL RESOURCES

(a) Grant Program	(b) Applicant	(c) State	(d) Other Sources	(e) TOTALS
8.	$	$	$	$
9.				
10.				
11.				
12. TOTAL (sum of lines 8-11)	$	$	$	$

SECTION D - FORECASTED CASH NEEDS

	Total for 1st Year	1st Quarter	2nd Quarter	3rd Quarter	4th Quarter
13. Federal	$	$	$	$	$
14. Non-Federal					
15. TOTAL (sum of lines 13 and 14)	$	$	$	$	$

Source: Grants.gov (2021), https://apply07.grants.gov/apply/forms/readonly/SF424A-V1.0.pdf

APPENDIX D

ADDITIONAL INFORMATION

THIS SECTION CONTAINS:

- Determining Percentage Change in Evaluation
- Sample Size Determination Using Krejcie and Morgan Table
- Program Design and Evaluation Case Study
- Government Requirements of GPRA
- Human Subjects Review Code of Regulations
- Sample Photographic Release
- Sample Informed Consent for Data Collection

DETERMINING PERCENTAGE CHANGE IN EVALUATION

The easiest type of indicator measure is knowledge change because you can give a pretest before the intervention to determine the amount of knowledge a person currently has and then give a posttest to determine the amount of knowledge the person has at the end of the service. In other words, you measure the knowledge of the individual at the start and again at the end. Hopefully, the person had a higher score (knew more) at the end than they did at the start of the service or program!

Here is a simple formula to determine percentage of change: 1) subtract the starting value from the ending value, 2) divide that number by the starting number, and 3) multiply by 100 to convert that rate to a percentage. Example: A student scored 82 points on the pretest and 92 points on the posttest. $92 - 82 = 10$. $10/82 = 0.1219 \times 100 = 12.19\%$ or simply 12%.)

SAMPLE SIZE DETERMINATION USING KREJCIE AND MORGAN TABLE

Small-Sample Techniques. (1960). *The NEA Research Bulletin*, Vol. 38.

N	S	N	S	N	S
10	10	220	140	1200	291
15	14	230	144	1300	297
20	19	240	148	1400	302
25	24	250	152	1500	306
30	28	260	155	1600	310
35	32	270	159	1700	313
40	36	280	162	1800	317
45	40	290	165	1900	320
50	44	300	169	2000	322
55	48	320	175	2200	327
60	52	340	181	2400	331
65	56	360	186	2600	335
70	59	380	191	2800	338
75	63	400	196	3000	341
80	66	420	201	3500	346
85	70	440	205	4000	351
90	73	460	210	4500	354
95	76	480	214	5000	357
100	80	500	217	6000	361
110	86	550	226	7000	364
120	92	600	234	8000	367
130	97	650	242	9000	368
140	103	700	248	10000	370
150	108	750	254	15000	375
160	113	800	260	20000	377
170	118	850	265	30000	379
180	123	900	269	40000	380
190	127	950	274	50000	381
200	132	1000	278	75000	382
210	136	1100	285	1000000	384

Note: N is population size. S is sample size.

Source: Krejcie & Morgan, 1970

PROGRAM DESIGN AND EVALUATION CASE STUDY

So that you might see how an evaluation plan becomes integrated into the program plan, let's begin with a hypothetical discussion: Let's say that my overall program goal is to prevent unintended adolescent pregnancy. I want to design a teen pregnancy prevention program for young adolescents. I am aware of the fact that this is a developmental period in which peers have a significant influence upon each other. As I read the professional literature, I find that *social learning* theory is one way to understand peer pressure and social norms. I select a curriculum for my program that is developed on the principles of social learning theory, and I design my program to include traditional classroom instruction, a teen theater component (the peer-to-peer aspect of social learning theory), a parent education component to improve parent and child communication, and a community advocacy component to address social norms promulgated through advertising and the media (again, a component of social learning theory). (Each of these program components will be written as measurable objectives.)

Then, as I am reading the program evaluation literature, I find the types of activities that have been used in the past in such programs and their success in reaching their goals. Suppose that I learn that the classroom educational component is more effective when provided by college-age adults as compared to teens or older adults, and consequently, I choose to design my educational intervention using college-age students. In this case, I can be said to be following *best practices* in that I am combining a sound theoretical orientation with a proven service delivery plan. I am now most likely to succeed.

GOVERNMENT REQUIREMENTS OF GPRA

The following description itemizes what the agency needs to provide to the federal government to comply with the Government Performance and Results Act of 1993 from the OMB. The website at Whitehouse.gov states:

Sec. 306. Strategic plans

(a) No later than September 30, 1997, the head of each agency shall submit to the Director of the Office of Management and Budget and to the Congress a strategic plan for program activities. Such plan shall contain—*(1) a comprehensive mission statement covering the major functions and operations of the agency; (2) general goals and objectives, including outcome-related goals and objectives, for the major functions and operations of the agency; (3) a description of how the goals and objectives are to be achieved, including a description of the operational processes, skills and technology, and the human, capital, information, and other resources required to meet those goals and objectives; (4) a description of how the performance goals included in the plan required by section 1115(a) of title 31 shall be related to the general goals and objectives in the strategic plan; (5) an identification of those key factors external to the agency and beyond its control that could significantly affect the achievement of the general goals and objectives; and (6) a description of the program evaluations used in establishing or revising general goals and objectives, with a schedule for future program evaluations.*

(b) The strategic plan shall cover a period of not less than five years forward from the fiscal year in which it is submitted, and shall be updated and revised at least every three years.

HUMAN SUBJECTS REVIEW CODE OF REGULATIONS

From HHS.gov:

Code of Federal Regulations
Title 45 Public Welfare

Section 46.101 To what does this policy apply?

(a) Except as provided in paragraph (b) of this section, this policy applies to all research involving human subjects conducted, supported, or otherwise subject to regulation by any federal department or agency which takes appropriate administrative action to make the policy applicable to such research. This includes research conducted by federal civilian employees or military personnel, except that each department or agency head may adopt such procedural modifications as may be appropriate from an administrative standpoint. It also includes research conducted, supported, or otherwise subject to regulation by the federal government outside the United States.

(1) Research that is conducted or supported by a federal department or agency, whether or not it is regulated as defined in §46.102, must comply with all sections of this policy.

(2) Research that is neither conducted nor supported by a federal department or agency but is subject to regulation as defined in §46.102(e) must be reviewed and approved, in compliance with §46.101, §46.102, and §46.107 through §46.117 of this policy, by an institutional review board (IRB) that operates in accordance with the pertinent requirements of this policy.

(b) Unless otherwise required by department or agency heads, research activities in which the only involvement of human subjects will be in one or more of the following categories are exempt from this policy:

(1) Research conducted in established or commonly accepted educational settings, involving normal educational practices, such as (i) research on regular and special education instructional strategies, or (ii) research on the effectiveness of or the comparison among instructional techniques, curricula, or classroom management methods.

(2) Research involving the use of educational tests (cognitive, diagnostic, aptitude, achievement), survey procedures, interview procedures, or observation of public behavior, unless:

(i) information obtained is recorded in such a manner that human subjects can be identified, directly or through identifiers linked to the subjects; and (ii) any disclosure of the human subjects' responses outside the research could reasonably place the subjects at risk of criminal or civil liability or be damaging to the subjects' financial standing, employability, or reputation.

(3) Research involving the use of educational tests (cognitive, diagnostic, aptitude, achievement), survey procedures, interview procedures, or observation of public behavior that is not exempt under paragraph (b)(2) of this section, if:

(i) the human subjects are elected or appointed public officials or candidates for public office; or (ii) federal statute(s) require(s) without exception that the confidentiality of the personally identifiable information will be maintained throughout the research and thereafter.

(4) Research involving the collection or study of existing data, documents, records, pathological specimens, or diagnostic specimens, if these sources are publicly available or if the information is recorded by the investigator in such a manner that subjects cannot be identified, directly or through identifiers linked to the subjects.

(5) Research and demonstration projects which are conducted by or subject to the approval of department or agency heads, and which are designed to study, evaluate, or otherwise examine:

   (i) Public benefit or service programs; (ii) procedures for obtaining benefits or services under those programs; (iii) possible changes in or alternatives to those programs or procedures; or (iv) possible changes in methods or levels of payment for benefits or services under those programs.

(6) Taste and food quality evaluation and consumer acceptance studies, (i) if wholesome foods without additives are consumed; or (ii) if a food is consumed that contains a food ingredient at or below the level and for a use found to be safe, or agricultural chemical or environmental contaminant at or below the level found to be safe, by the Food and Drug Administration or approved by the Environmental Protection Agency or the Food Safety and Inspection Service of the U.S. Department of Agriculture.

(c) Department or agency heads retain final judgment as to whether a particular activity is covered by this policy.

(d) Department or agency heads may require that specific research activities or classes of research activities conducted, supported, or otherwise subject to regulation by the department or agency but not otherwise covered by this policy, comply with some or all of the requirements of this policy.

(e) Compliance with this policy requires compliance with pertinent federal laws or regulations which provide additional protections for human subjects.

(f) This policy does not affect any state or local laws or regulations which may otherwise be applicable and which provide additional protections for human subjects.

(g) This policy does not affect any foreign laws or regulations which may otherwise be applicable and which provide additional protections to human subjects of research.

(h) When research covered by this policy takes place in foreign countries, procedures normally followed in the foreign countries to protect human subjects may differ from those set forth in this policy. [An example is a foreign institution which complies with guidelines consistent with the World Medical Assembly Declaration (Declaration of Helsinki amended 1989) issued either by sovereign states or by an organization whose function for the protection of human research subjects is internationally recognized.] In these circumstances, if a department or agency head determines that the procedures prescribed by the institution afford protections that are at least equivalent to those provided in this policy, the department or agency head may approve the substitution of the foreign procedures in lieu of the procedural requirements provided in this policy. Except when otherwise required by statute, Executive Order, or the department or agency head, notices of these actions as they occur will be published in the FEDERAL REGISTER or will be otherwise published as provided in department or agency procedures.

(i) Unless otherwise required by law, department or agency heads may waive the applicability of some or all of the provisions of this policy to specific research activities or classes or research activities otherwise covered by this policy. Except when otherwise required by statute or Executive Order, the department or agency head shall forward advance notices of these actions to the Office for Human Research Protections, Department of Health and Human Services (HHS), or any successor office, and shall also publish them in the FEDERAL REGISTER or in such other manner as provided in department or agency procedures.[1]

---

[1] Institutions with HHS-approved assurances on file will abide by provisions of Title 45 CFR part 46 subparts A–D. Some of the other departments and agencies have incorporated all provisions of Title 45 CFR part 46 into their policies and procedures as well. However, the exemptions at 45 CFR 46.101(b) do not apply to research involving prisoners, subpart C. The exemption at 45 CFR 46.101(b)(2), for research involving survey or interview procedures or observation of public behavior, does not apply to research with children, subpart D, except for research involving observations of public behavior when the investigator(s) do not participate in the activities being observed.

SAMPLE PHOTOGRAPHIC RELEASE

(We provide these samples to you for you to realize that these are needed and to encourage you to develop a release using this format on agency letterhead [if none exist] and take it to an attorney prior to use.)

The Geta Grant agency is asking your permission to photograph, video, or audio record you and/or your children. We will use the photos, videos, or sound recordings in our brochures, newsletters, annual reports, or other printed or audio materials that we develop to advertise our services, report to our donors and community, and report to our funders. The agency may place these images in publications that we sell. **You (or your children) will receive no financial or program advantage by agreeing to participate in the photographs, videos, or audio recordings.**

We need your permission to use any photo, movie, or voice recording. When you sign below, you give us your permission.

———————————————   ———————————————

Name   Date

———————————————   ———————————————

Address   City and Zip

———————————————   ———————————————

Phone   Email

———————————————   ———————————————

Name of Minor Child   Your Permission-Sign here

SAMPLE INFORMED CONSENT FOR DATA COLLECTION

Informed Consent Form

Title of this study:

Project team:

You are being asked to participate in a data collection/needs assessment study.

Before you agree to take part in this study, Dr./Mr./Ms. _____

or his/her representative will tell you:

- Why the study is being done and what will happen to you if you take part in the study: [insert brief explanation]

- How long you will be in the study: [insert brief explanation]

- How many people will be in the study: [insert estimate]

- The possible foreseeable risks, discomforts, and benefits of this study: [insert brief explanation]

- How your study records will be maintained and who will have access: [insert brief explanation]

- If you will be compensated for taking part in this study: [insert brief explanation]

- How the data will be used: [insert brief explanation]

If you agree to participate in this study, you will be given a signed copy of this document.

You may contact Dr./Mr./Ms._____at (xxx) xxx-xx-xx [insert number here] at any time if you have questions about the study or if you think that you have been hurt by the study.

You may choose not to be in this study, or you may quit being in the study at any time, and there will be no penalty and no loss of any benefits you are entitled to.

Information collected about you will be stored in locked filing cabinets or in computers with security passwords. Only certain people have the legal right to review these research records, and they will protect the secrecy (confidentiality) of these records as much as the law allows. Otherwise your records will not be released without your permission unless required by law or a court order.

Once this research study is completed, any information that could identify you **might** be removed from any identifiable private information collected and, after such removal, the information could be used for future research studies or distributed to another investigator for future research studies without additional informed consent from you or your legally authorized representative.

The study team will take appropriate steps to protect any information they collect about you. However, there is a slight risk that information about you could be revealed inappropriately or accidentally. Depending on the nature of the information, such a release could upset or embarrass you or possibly even affect your insurability or employability.

If the results of this study are published or presented at meetings or documents, your identity will not be disclosed.

Signing this document means that the study, including the above information, has been described to you orally and/or that you have read this document, and you voluntarily agree to take part.

_____   _____
Signature of Person Obtaining Consent   Date

_____   _____
Signature of Person Consenting   Date

PROPOSAL SECTIONS

THE LETTER OF INTENT

The purpose of the letter of intent is to inform the funder as to what your proposed project is about in the hope that the funder will be interested in the program and allow you to submit a full proposal. You should enclose enough detail so that the funder can see the details of the project as well as the rationale for the project. It is a good idea to show this letter to a friend and ask them if the proposed project is clear and if it sounds interesting and exciting to them. Try to keep the letter to one to two pages or to the length requested by the funder.

Sample Letter of Intent (on agency letterhead)

Dear Funder:

The XYZ Agency is pleased to apply for funding under Application PO71652 for Funding Community Health Initiatives in Hispanic Populations. XYZ Agency has 26 years of experience providing health programs and services to the Hispanic/Latino population in Whatchamacallit County, PA. Local area research indicates that our 580,000-member population is most in need of prevention services in diabetes and hypertension because these two disease areas represent 80% of the cause of death to adults and are caused primarily by obesity. Food preferences and activity levels are mostly set in childhood, and accordingly, our project focuses on children and young adults in an effort to prevent these conditions.

Project AYUDA brings a unique strategy to bear: 1) activity offerings that meet cultural preferences such as soccer, folkloric dancing, and bike riding; 2) cooking classes during which the youth cook and serve their families reduced-calorie versions of family favorites; and 3) educational information on diabetes and heart disease. Four cohorts of 30 children and young adults in this project will meet after school, 5 days a week for 6 weeks over the course of this 9-month (school-year) project.

At the completion of the project, we expect that the children and young adults who were overweight at the beginning will have lost weight (a 25% reduction in weight) and will have increased exercise by 20% over the previous level. We also expect the participants and their families to increase their knowledge of diabetes and heart disease prevention by 20%. In addition, we will evaluate the program's capacity to change behaviors long term and expect that the families will adopt the new, reduced-calorie recipes for daily use in their homes.

The total budget request is $209,827. We look forward to your reply.

Sincerely,

Executive Director

THE COVER LETTER

A letter of transmittal on agency stationery, signed by the appropriate organizational official, should convey interest in the funder's mandate and mission and state how the project fits within these mandates. The letter should be brief (usually one page); it should indicate the agency's board approval of the proposal; the contact person, with telephone number; the amount requested; and the willingness to respond to any questions about the project. Also, include a paragraph that summarizes the project as well.

Remember that the letter is often the first contact between the agency requesting funds and the prospective funder. Set a tone of professionalism and competency. The letter should be written on agency letterhead.

Sample Cover Letter (on agency letterhead):

Dear Mr./Ms. Funding Officer (if you know it) or Dear Formal Business Name of the Funding Agency (Dear U. S. Department of Health):

The XYZ Agency is pleased to submit this application for funding under PA714532 School and Community Safety. The project, called AYUDA, means *help* in Spanish and represents the culmination of 6 years of collaborative efforts among the XYZ Agency, the Putnam School District, and the Boys and Girls Clubs of Putnam County. We are alarmed that up to 80% of our local program population will develop Type 2 diabetes and/or heart disease by the age of 50 (Grant County Health Statistics, 2014). Our partnership (with the XYZ Agency serving as lead agency) has crafted a project using local data and best practices known to positively affect the health issues we target and improve the health outcomes in our community.

Project AYUDA will offer culturally appropriate and exciting counseling, educational health services and sports and activities through after-school and evening programs at the school and the Boys and Girls Club. The program will improve the health status of 120 children, ages 10 to 13, and their families (a total of at least 400 persons). In addition, it will reach broadly into the Hispanic community with information and pubic events designed to improve the knowledge and activity levels of the community as a whole. We will measure the program's success with using pre- and posttesting of educational attainment, health status measures, and reports of exercise behavioral change. The total cost of the project is $209,827.

We are happy to respond to any questions you may have and look forward to hearing from you.

Sincerely,

Executive Director	Executive Director	Superintendent
XYZ Agency	Boys and Girls Clubs	Putnam School District
(888) 899–0987	(888) 899–6789	(888) 567–8765

THE TITLE AND TITLE PAGE

Most funders will require you to provide a title for the project. You will want to develop a title that reflects the major focus of the project. One may develop a catchy title, like one where the project's acronym spells something meaningful, for example: Project HOPE (Homeless Outreach to Persons in Encampments) or a descriptive title like Ayuda, where the meaning of the project should be readily understood by the reviewers. A descriptive subtitle might be used to clarify, for example, Ayuda: Bringing Healthy Living. Avoid long titles or ones that are used too often by other projects in your area so as not to get your program confused with another.

A title page usually accompanies the proposal. Federal and state agencies will often provide the face sheets necessary. Although there is no standard format for the title page, the following is typical:

Project Title:

Name of the Agency Submitting Grant:

Agency Address:

Name of Prospective Funder:

Project Start and End Dates:

Amount Requested:

Sample Title Page

Agency Name: XYZ Agency   Date: November 15, 20xx

Project ID: PA714532 School and Community Safety

Project Name: AYUDA

Fiscal Agency: XYZ Agency   Contact: Ann Martinez, Executive Director

Address: 2172 Main Street Whatchamacallit, PA 87765

Phone: (888) 333-9876   Email: am@xyzagency.org Fax: (888) 333-9877

Submitted to: United States Department of Education

Anticipated Project Term: October 1, 2025 to September 30, 2026

Request: $209,827

THE PROPOSAL ABSTRACT

The abstract is written after the other sections are complete because it gives an overview of the entire project. A funder usually stipulates the number of words the abstract should contain, often 100 to 500 words. If, in the unlikely event that the funder does not provide instructions or forms, the abstract should be kept to less than one page. The abstract is used by the funder to screen the proposal for appropriateness in light of their funding objectives and assists staff in disseminating the document for review. Once a proposal is funded, the abstract is often used in establishing a contract number as well as to convey grantee information and activities to both internal and external constituents.

Although the abstract is sometimes hurriedly written at the end, you should give care and attention to its development. It is difficult to bring a clear and concise description of the project in so few words, and it takes careful crafting. Remember, this is a complete summary of the entire project, and as such, it should parallel the major sections of the proposal. An abstract will typically do the following:

- Identify the agency requesting the funds,

- Describe the target population,

- Summarize the needs/problem statement highlighting data which show the magnitude or extent of the problem,

- Provide a synopsis of the project objectives including goals and objectives,

- Highlight the evaluation plan and the expected outcomes or results of the project, and

- Provide an "amount requested" figure.

Sample Project Abstract (Max 100 Words)

Project AYUDA by XYZ Agency, the Putnam School District, and Boys and Girls Clubs will reduce precursors to Type 2 diabetes and heart disease in 400 persons in a high-risk, Hispanic community. (Persons in this low-income community have an 80% greater risk of Type 2 diabetes and heart disease than higher-income areas.) The program targets youth, ages 10 to 13, and their parents with health services/assessments, counseling, nutrition planning, and after-school activities. Parents meet monthly to encourage outdoor activity. Participants will improve health by 25% (weight reduction, activity, access to health care) by project end. Request is $209,827.

LOGIC MODEL SAMPLE

Logic Model of Veteran Reentry

Objective: Support reentry of veterans into workforce as public relations and communications professionals through academic training and coaching.				
Inputs	**Activities**	**Outputs**	**Outcomes**	**Impact**
(What we have/need)	(What we do)	(What we observe)	(What we measure)	(Our goal)
Program coordinators	*Training*	**Number** of veterans trained	*Short term*	Reentry of veterans into workforce
Curriculum	-PR campaigns		Gain in communication skills	
Volunteer academic coaches	-Public speaking	**Number** of coaching sessions	Gain in positive job outlook	
	-Media relations			
Internship sites	*Coaching*	**Number** of internship placements	*Intermediate*	
	-Personal strengths		Increase in veteran reemployment rate	
	-Networking			
	-Job orientation			
	Internship			
	-3 x 4-week rotations			
	-Portfolio development			

APPENDIX F

HANDOUT MATERIALS

THIS SECTION CONTAINS:

- Instructor Materials
- Chapter 2: Concept Mapping
- Chapter 3: Funding Search
- Chapter 4: Needs and Solutions
- Chapter 5: Writing a persuasive Statement
- Chapter 6: Estimating Resources Needed
- Chapter 7: Needs Analysis
- Chapter 7: Logic Model Template
- Chapter 7: Program Activities and Outcomes Mapping
- Chapter 8: Theory of Change
- Chapter 9: Sample GANTT Chart
- Chapter 9: Scope of Work Form
- Chapter 10: Budget Questions Activity
- Chapter 11: Developing a Project Name or Title
- Chapter 11: Writing a Project Abstract Activity

INSTRUCTOR MATERIALS

End-of-chapter questions can be used as individual and group in-class activities. They can also be used as take-home assignments. Instructor guidelines presented in this appendix include learning objectives aligned with the Bloom's taxonomy levels of learning, full-page handouts for several end-of-chapter activities, and a grading rubric for activities as individual assignments.

Bloom's Taxonomy Levels

Learning Objective	Definition
Level 1: Remembering	Exhibit memory of previously learned material by recalling facts, terms, basic concepts, and answers.
Level 2: Understanding	Demonstrate understanding of facts and ideas by organizing, comparing, translating, interpreting, giving descriptions, and stating main ideas.
Level 3: Applying	Solve problems to new situations by applying acquired knowledge, facts, techniques, and rules in a different way.
Level 4: Analyzing	Examine and break information into parts by identifying motives or causes. Make inferences and find evidence to support generalizations.
Level 5: Evaluating	Present and defend opinions by making judgments about information, validity of ideas, or quality of work based on a set of criteria.
Level 6: Creating	Compile information together in a different way by combining elements in a new pattern or proposing alternative solutions.

Learning Objectives for the End-of-Chapter Activities

Chapter	Learning Objectives
1	Activity 1: Define grant writing skills and tasks (Level 1) Activity 2: Identify proposal-writing tasks (Level 3)
2	Activity 1: Compare mission and vision statements of sponsors and grant seekers (Level 2) Activity 2: Identify similarities and differences in funding needs and priorities (Level 5).
3	Activity 1: Find and compare grant funding opportunities (Levels 1&2)

4	Activity 1: Identify proposal components of a specific RFA (Level 3)
	Activity 2: Formulate an initial proposal idea (Level 6)
	Activity 3: List community needs and identify project ideas (Levels 1&4)
5	Activity 1: Construct and evaluate project goals and activities (Levels 3&5)
	Activity 2: Outline a proposal (Level 2)
	Activity 3: Identify and assess collaboration opportunities (Levels 3&5)
6	Activity 1: Define and explain existing community needs (Level 1&2)
	Activity 2: Examine and defend proposal needs (Level 5)
	Activity 3: Analyze the factors that contribute to the project need (Level 4)
7	Activity 1: Outline and create a logic model (Levels 2&6)
	Activity 2: Categorize project activities and outcomes (Level 4)
8	Activity 1: Formulate and evaluate project needs (Levels 5&6)
	Activity 2: Develop a project need statement (Level 6)
9	Activity 1: Analyze and assess project scope and required inputs (Levels 4&5)
	Activity 2: Estimate project timeline (Level 5)
10	Activity 1: Construct a model proposal budget (Level 3)
	Activity 2: Estimate project costs (Level 6)
11	Activity 1: Construct and evaluate proposal abstract (Levels 3&5)
	Activity 2: Identify and invite a collaborator (Levels 3&4).

Discussion Post Guidelines

Most end-of-chapter activities can be used as take-home assignments and/or discussion posts. Below is a sample discussion post guideline.

Your response should be at least a paragraph (three to five well-constructed sentences) that cogently responds to one of the questions/statements and draws on both your own experience and the concepts in the textbook and lectures as appropriate. You also need to post a response to one of your classmates asking them to analyze, critique, and provide suggestions.

CHAPTER 2: CONCEPT MAPPING

Agency 1 Core Concepts

_____   _____   _____

Agency 2 Core Concepts

_____   _____   _____

Agency 3 Core Concepts

_____   _____   _____

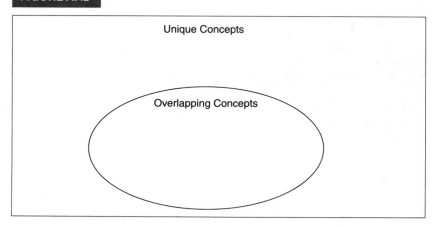

FIGURE AF.1

Unique Concepts

Overlapping Concepts

CHAPTER 3: FUNDING SEARCH

Key words: _____ AND/OR _____

_____ AND/OR _____

_____ AND/OR _____

Search Results:

Sponsor name	
Funding opportunity description	
Deadline	

Sponsor name	
Funding opportunity description	
Deadline	

Sponsor name	
Funding opportunity description	
Deadline	

CHAPTER 4: NEEDS AND SOLUTIONS

Problems/Needs   Ideas to Address Problems

CHAPTER 5: WRITING A PERSUASIVE STATEMENT

1. Imagine that you are a substitute teacher writing a request to purchase a new iPhone that has the ability to translate your speech into any language and a reply back into English. The phone will have an instant impact on classroom learning. You need to write a short (four- to six-sentence) paragraph that describes the phone and convinces the school principal to purchase it.

2. Share this with your class or friend to get their feedback. Did they become interested in the phone? Did it persuade them to buy one? What did you learn about writing a persuasive paragraph in this exercise?

CHAPTER 6: ESTIMATING RESOURCES NEEDED

1. Estimate Staffing Costs

Staff Position	Estimated Yearly Amount
Total	

2. Estimate Operational Costs

Item	Estimated Yearly Amount
Total	

CHAPTER 7: NEEDS ANALYSIS

1. What is/are the needs/problems/issues you wish to address?

2. What is the magnitude of the current problem/need/issue? Over what period of time?

    -   What reliable data sources would best depict the magnitude of the need/problem/issue?

    -   What are the direct and indirect impacts on individuals/ groups/ community/society?

    -   Are there differentials among groups (e.g. ethnic, gender, age, income, education)?

3. What are the multitude of factors that contribute to the need/problem/ issue? Identify in each category (as applicable):

Individual & Family Factors	
Community & Environmental Factors	
Institutional Factors	
Systemic & Societal Factors	

4. What is the vision or desired state if this need/problem/issue is addressed?

5. What are the circumstances or conditions that would make this problem/ need/issue nonexistent? What is the desired state?

CHAPTER 7: LOGIC MODEL TEMPLATE

Inputs	Activities	Outputs	Outcomes	Impact
			Short-term	
			Intermediate	

CHAPTER 7: PROGRAM ACTIVITIES AND OUTCOMES MAPPING

Outcome   Activities   Resources

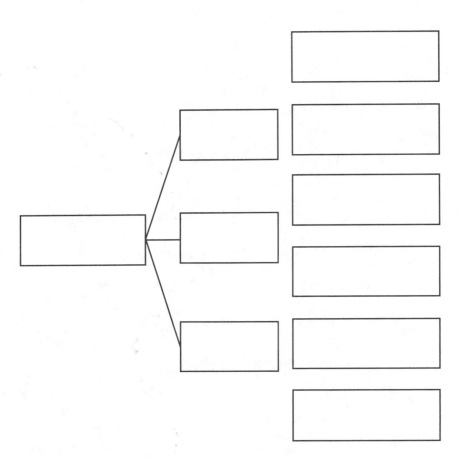

CHAPTER 8: THEORY OF CHANGE

Although it sounds complex, it is quite easy to articulate the theory of change that undergirds your project. Everything you have designed tells us the theory of change. Here are a few questions to help you identify your theory of change.

1. What is the specific problem you are addressing?

2. What does the research say about what is causing this problem?

3. What other programs have addressed this problem, and how successful were they?

4. Show how your program is designed after the most successful program designs in the field (and, if not, why not?).

5. Voilá, you have just articulated your theory of change!

CHAPTER 9: SAMPLE GANTT CHART TEMPLATE

Major Project Milestones	Year 1				Year 2				Year 3			
	Q1	Q2	Q3	Q4	Q1	Q2	Q3	Q4	Q1	Q2	Q3	Q4

CHAPTER 9: SCOPE OF WORK FORM

1. What is the overarching goal(s) for this project?

    Goal 1:

    Goal 2:

    Goal 3:

2. Taking the first goal from the above list, provide two measurable objectives:

    Goal 1: Objective 1:

    Goal 2: Objective 2:

3. Continue using the first goal and objective and write at least three implementation activities:

1.1 A:

1.1 B:

1.1 C:

CHAPTER 10: BUDGET QUESTIONS ACTIVITY

1. A full-time employee is estimated to work a total of 2,080 hours per year. How many hours would a half-time employee work?

    _____

    How would you write the FTE for a half-time employee?

    _____

2. Your total program budget is $50,000 to provide 10 hours of tutoring to 10 students.

    What is the cost per student?

    What is the cost per hour per student?

    Does this seem like a reasonable cost per client?

3. What is the total budget for your project?

    How many clients are there, and what do they receive?

    What is the cost per client?

    What is the cost per hour or item per client?

    Does this seem like a reasonable cost per client to you?

4. When you think of your project, which budget items could possibly be donated (e.g., think printing, professional services, or office supplies)? Make a list of the items and their estimated costs. How much does this reduce the total budget?

5. Write two to three sentences for each of the above costs to describe and justify these budget items.

Answers:

1. 1,040, 0.50 FTE, or 50% time

2. $5,000 per student and $500 per hour. Not a reasonable cost.

CHAPTER 11: DEVELOPING A PROJECT NAME OR TITLE

Most grant programs have a specific funding title with the funder and a number, but in addition to this, the project is given a name. Usually, the name fits the main theme of the funding. For example, programs in Orlando, Florida, designed to improve family involvement with health care systems might be called Orlando Healthy Families. An education program might choose to use an acronym like FACT standing for Families and Communities Together. You don't want to get too cute with the name—keep it simple and short for the best results.

1. What is a possible name for your project?

2. Is there any way that people might misunderstand this name? Think of Chevrolet when they named their car Nova. Hispanic's avoided the vehicle because in Spanish the name meant "doesn't go" or *no va*!

3. Test the name out on family and friends to see if they like it and would use it.

CHAPTER 11: WRITING A PROJECT ABSTRACT ACTIVITY

Create and "Elevator Pitch" Challenge yourself to explain your project in one to two minutes or roughly the amount of time it would take to tell a stranger about the project riding from the first to the second floor on an elevator.

1. What is the goal of the project?

2. What is the agency name that is hosting this project?

3. How many clients will be served, and what will they get?

4. Are there any unique features about this project?

5. How will you know if the project is successful?

6. How much does the total project cost?

REFERENCES AND SUGGESTED READINGS

American Red Cross. (2016). *Mission and values*. http://www.redcross.org/about-us/who-we-are/mission-and-values

Bandura, A. (1986). *Social foundations of thought and action: A social cognitive theory*. Prentice Hall.

Boys & Girls Clubs of America. (n.d.). Frequently asked questions. https://www.bgca.org/about-us/faqs#two

Brewer, E., Achilles, C., Fuhriman, J., & Hollingsworth, C. (2001). *Finding funding: Grantwriting from start to finish, including project management and Internet use* (4th ed.). Corwin.

Burke, M. A. (2002). *Simplified grantwriting*. Corwin.

Carr, C. E. (2015). *The nuts and bolts of grant writing*. Sage.

Diamond, H. (1998). A perfect union: Public-private partnerships can provide valuable services. *National Parks Forum, 40*(4).

Casagrande, J. (2010). *It was the best of sentences, it was the worst of sentences*. Ten Speed Press.

Clark, R. P. (2013). *Help! for writers: 210 solutions to the problems every writer faces*. Little, Brown.

Dictionary.com. (n.d.). *Philanthropy*. In Dictionary.com. http://dictionary.reference.com/browse/philanthropy

Dluhy, M., & Kravitz, S. (1990). *Building coalitions in the human services*. Sage.

Encyclopedia Britannica. (2012). Poor law. In *Encyclopedia Britannica online*. http://www.britannica.com/EBchecked/topic/469923/Poor-Law

Etymology Dictionary. (n.d.). Philanthropy. In *Online Etymology Dictionary*. https://www.etymonline.com/word/philanthropy.

Foundation Directory Online. (n.d.). http://www.FoundationCenter.org

Gantt Chart. (n.d.). https://en.wikipedia.org/wiki/Gantt_chart

Gardner, S. (1999). *Beyond collaboration to results: Hard choices in the future of services to children and families*. California State University, Center for Collaboration for Children.

GrantCraft: A Service of the Foundation Center. (n.d.). http://www.grantcraft.org

Grants.gov. (n.d.) U.S. federal grant announcement portal. https://www.grants.gov/web/grants/search-grants.html

Gilman, A. (1995). *Get to the point: How to say what you mean and get what you want*. Kendall Hunt.

Giving USA. (2020). Giving USA 2020. https://givingusa.org/giving-usa-2020-charitable-giving-showed-solid-growth-climbing-to-449-64-billion-in-2019-one-of-the-highest-years-for-giving-on-record/

Hatry, H. (1996). *Measuring program outcomes: A practical approach* (4th ed.). United Way of America.

Internal Revenue Service (IRS). (2016, April 4). Forms and publications. https://www.irs.gov/Forms-&-Pubs

Kenya Projects Organization. (n.d.). http://www.KENPRO.org

Kettner, P. M., & Martin, L. L. (1987). *Purchase of service contracting*. Sage.

Kettner, P. M., & Martin, L. L. (1996). *Measuring the performance of human service programs*. Sage.

Kettner, P., Moroney R., & Martin, L. (2016). *Designing and managing programs: An effectiveness-based approach*. Sage.

Kiritz, N. J. (1980). *Program planning and proposal writing*. The Grantsmanship Center.

Kniffel, A. (1995). Corporate sponsorship: The new direction in fundraising. *American Libraries, 26*(10), 1023–1026.

Knowlton, L., & Phillips, C. (2009). *The logic model guidebook: Better strategies for great results.* Sage.

Krejcie, R. V., & Morgan, D. W. (1970). Determining sample size for research activities. *Educational and Psychological Measurement, 30*(3), 607–610.

Lauffer, A. (1997). *Grants, etc.—grant getting, contracting and fund-raising for non-profits.* Sage.

Melaville, A. (1997). *A guide to selecting results and indicators: Implementing results-based budgeting.* The Finance Project.

National Center for Charitable Statistics. (2020a). The Urban Institute. http://nccs.urban.org/statistics/quickfacts.cfm

National Center for Charitable Statistics. (2020b). *The nonprofit sector in brief.* The Urban Institute. https://nccs.urban.org/project/nonprofit-sector-brief

National Council of Nonprofits. (2019). Nonprofit impact matters: How America's charitable nonprofits strengthen communities and improve lives. https://www.nonprofitimpactmatters.org/site/assets/files/1/nonprofit-impact-matters-sept-2019-1.pdf

Netting, F. E., & Williams, F. G. (1997). Is there an afterlife? How to move towards self-sufficiency when foundation dollars end. *Nonprofit Management & Leadership, 7*(3), 291–304.

Peterson, S. (2001). *The grantwriter's Internet companion.* Corwin.

Roth, J., Brooks-Gunn, J., Murray, L., & Foster, W. (1998). Promoting healthy adolescents: Synthesis of youth development program evaluations. *Journal of Research on Adolescence 8*(4), 423–459.

Ruskin, K., & Achilles, C. (1995). *Grantwriting, fundraising, and partnerships: Strategies that work!* Corwin.

Schaefer, M. (1987). *Implementing change in service programs.* Sage.

Schorr, L. (1995). *The case for shifting to results-based accountability.* Center for the Study of Social Policy.

Schram, B. (1997). *Creating small scale social programs.* Sage.

Soriano, F. I. (1995). *Conducting needs assessments: A multidisciplinary approach.* Sage.

Sternberg, R. J. (2014). *Writing successful grant proposals from the top down and bottom up.* Sage.

Thayer, K. (2012, January 25). Hull House closing Friday. *Chicago Tribune.* http://articles.chicagotribune.com/2012-01-25/news/ct-met-hull-house-20120126_1_child-care-union-contract-employees

The Weather Channel. (2021). Mission. https://weather.com/mission

UC Berkeley Public Health Library. (n.d.). http://www.llib.berkeley.edu/PUBL/grans.html

U.S. Department of Health and Human Services Division of Grants. (2016). *Get ready for grants management.* http://www.hhs.gov/grants/grants/get-ready/index.html

Vinter, R. D., & Kish, R. K. (1984). *Budgeting for not-for-profit organizations.* The Free Press.

Young, N., Gardner, S., & Coley, S. (1994). Getting to outcomes in integrated service delivery models. In *Making a difference: Moving to outcome-based accountability for comprehensive service reforms* (National Center on Service Integration Service Brief 7). National Center for Service Integration.

INDEX